New Panchayati Raj System At Work

ABOUT THE AUTHOR

Ganapathy Palanithurai is an academic activist and a staunch supporter of grass-root democracy and alternative approach of development. He is currently heading the Department of Political Science and Development Administration in Gandhigram Rural University and Professor in Rajiv Gandhi Chair for Panchayati Raj Studies. His active intervention at the policy-making level is felt and his services are utilised by Government of Tamil Nadu through its Planning Commission, Population Foundation, New Delhi, Government of India through its Ministry of Rural Areas and Employment for activating grass-root democracy. He has to his credit twenty-two books, seventy articles in reputed journals, nine working papers, seven monographs on three major areas : Legislative Behaviour, Ethnicity and Panchayati Raj System. At present, he is involved in capacitation of elected representatives of the people in the local bodies. So far, he has trained more than one thousand two hundred Urban local body women leaders and six hundred rural local body leaders. He has evolved training module and manual for Local body leaders. His endeavours are supported by NGO's, both federal and state governments apart from Rajiv Gandhi Foundation and Population Foundation of India. He was awarded the "Junior Fellow" of the World Academy of Art and Science, USA and "Man of the Year 1998" of American Biographical Institute, USA. He was awarded a fellowship by Shastri Indo-Canadian Institute, New Delhi to write a book on "Comparative Ethnicity".

New Panchayati Raj System At Work : An Evaluation

G. PALANITHURAI
Rajiv Gandhi Chair for Panchayati Raj Studies
Deptt. of Political Science and Development Administration
The Gandhigram Rural Institute Deemed University
Gandhigram (T.N.)

CONCEPT PUBLISHING COMPANY, NEW DELHI - 110059

ISBN-81-7022-767-4

First Published 1999

Published and Printed by
Ashok Kumar Mittal
Concept Publishing Company
A/15-16, Commercial Block, Mohan Garden
NEW DELHI-110 059

Phones : 5648039, 5649024
Fax : 091-11-5648053

PREFACE

Governance is redefined, economy is globalised, and power is decentralized with an objective of accelerating economic growth and achieving equity. Government is not a provider but a facilitator. Planning process has undergone a tumultuous change from top-down to bottom-up. Multifaceted activities are on to integrate the micro unit of democracy with National Political System to achieve economic development and social justice. The above posited steps ought to have arrested the expansion of government by its structure, proliferation of schemes and programmes from the federal and state governments, and centralization of powers. Even after five years of the enactment of the 73rd Amendment to the Constitution of India one could not see the alternative process of planning as per 243 (G) of the act as the old mind set of the policy makers continue to stay on in the traditional mode of planning. People believe that the new panchayati system is going to proliferate more number of schemes as state and central governments. Federal and state governments have allocated rupees one crore and twenty-five lakhs to members of Parliament and Legislative Assembly respectively every year to administer development. Yet activities are going on in the rural areas for administering development through the new panchayati raj system. Legislation has been made, rules have been framed, Government orders have been issued to demarcate powers and responsibilities to different tiers of the system, resources have been allocated to local bodies and yet the basic questions remain unanswered. Are local body institutions really self governing? Do they plan for development from the below? Do they involve people in the process of development?

To find answers to the above stated questions, a study has been undertaken in the Rajiv Gandhi Chair for Panchayati Raj Studies in the Gandhigram Rural Institute. The outcome of the study is the present book. Tamil Nadu is known for the enactment of a most backward act with regard to New Panchayati Raj System. The inquiry is centered around the functioning of the local bodies and as to what extent the local bodies are functioning in line with the spirit of the 73rd constitutional Amendment Act. All the aspects of the local bodies have been deeply examined from the enactment of the act to the day-to-day affairs and activities of the panchayati institutions, and cases have been projected to demonstrate the reality.

It is self evident from the cases projected in this work that local body institutions have been made as agencies to implement the schemes and programmes of the federal and state governments. Logically speaking the centralized schemes have to be reduced and localized schemes evolved from the below have to be increased. Enough resources have to be provided to local bodies to meet the needs apart from the resources to be mobilized by the local bodies on their own. Contract system has to be removed and instead people involved implementation has to be initiated. Personnel, who are working in the local bodies, are accountable to the local bodies and more directly to the people. Women, though new to the office, have to be empowered to act independently and for which a support base has to be created. Likewise the *dalits* have to exercise their options as they like, to administer development and social justice.

All these issues have been visualised from the

perspective of the 73rd amendment to the Constitution of India, perception of the development functionaries, political will of the leaders of the province, and belief system of the people over the new system of Governance at the grass-root level. Inferences have been arrived at from the cases projected. Examinations have been done from the village level to district level as an integrated unit. The interface between the state government and the local bodies has also been investigated. Many issues have been examined. Since it is explored with an objective of providing information to the common readers on the new panchayati raj system, complicated jargons have been avoided. Events and issues have been projected in simple terms with a descriptive analysis.

Any work is an outcome of a team work in our chair. Though I have given framework, massive information have been collected by our team. They include Thiruvalargal M.A. Thirunavukkarasu, M. Gurusamy, S. Devaraj, A. Thangathurai and G. Umashankar. Their contributions are laudable and they deserve appreciation. Equally my colleague Mr. V. Ragupathy deserves a special mention here for his constant and consistent assistance to me to complete this work and to perform my academic duty.

The Gram Panchayat presidents, Block Panchayat presidents and District Panchayat presidents, officials working in different offices administering development have spared their valuable time with our research team for providing information need a special mention here. They are plain in their interaction, open in their observation and specific in their evaluation about the functioning of the local bodies. Their interactions are always suggestive. They interacted freely with the research team with the hope that our exercise will bring some positive changes in the mind set of the top officials.

Yet another unit which needs a special mention here is my family. My wife Mrs. Mala and my kids Senthil Vadivu and Aurobindh, for their keen attention in doing their respective activities which in turn helped me a lot to complete my work with concentration and without any disturbance. Hence I place on record my sense of gratitude to them. My typist Mr. G. Rajan has always been co-operative and neat in his execution of work and more so in time. He deserves my appreciation. Finally for the publication which evinced keen interest in Panchayati Raj System by bringing out more number of books on Local bodies and in this respect Concept Publication deserves our appreciation.

Gandhigram
10th March, 1998

G. Palanithurai

CONTENTS

LIST OF TABLES

1

NEW PANCHAYATI RAJ SYSTEM AND ITS IMPLICATIONS

Introduction

New Panchayati Raj System is the outcome of the world-wide movement to liberate the people from the clutches of the big government and the total state system. It is also one of the new policy options of Rajiv Gandhi to integrate our system of political and economic activities with the activities of the developed societies. The new arrangement of decentralization of power or devolution of power or empowerment of people is equated to developing resourcefulness of the people or entrustment of more responsibilities to the people and to turn the government from the role of a provider to facilitator and by which the role and function of the government will be reduced and the role of government in the present context has to be redefined. Success of any system needs a thorough understanding of the system by the operator. Hence to make the new Panchayati Raj System vibrant and active, the people are to be made aware of the full implications of the new system. The new system envisages more of responsibilities rather than powers and authority.

The Problem

It is unequivocal that the Government of India or for that matter any state government are not in a position to make a statement that they have provided basic minimum facilities to the people of India for a reasonably decent life which is required for a human being in a democratic country. The fifty years of democratic governance through our parliamentary institutions has achieved substantially in many fields at the macro level but these macro achievements have not altered the life style of the people at the micro level. The micro realities have compelled the planners and policy makers to think of new arrangements to meet the challenges in the rural societies which are the backbone of our social and political systems of our country. The new arrangement of New Panchayati Raj System is to administer development by involving people in every stage of the development process, utilising the skill available with them, and using the natural resources available in their areas. It is not only for growth but also for equity and social justice.

Characteristics of the New System

The concept, panchayat has its own antiquity and ambiguity in the minds of all as it is seen from the backdrop of histriography. It should be seen contextually and more particularly in the background of the policy packages of the federal and state governments and the ongoing development process of the world. The new system has been given a constitutional status and by which it has got permanence in the Indian Political System as a third government. It has a three-tier structural arrangement namely, district panchayat, middle level Panchayat and Gram Panchayat. This new system has been vested with the power of taking decision on twenty-nine subjects in the 11th Schedule. To alter the planning process of the country, a statutory planning body—District Planning Committee—has been created at the district level. To maintain periodicity in conducting election to local bodies, State Election Commission has been created and by which it is declared that election will be conducted to local bodies regularly in every five years and even if the local bodies are dissolved and dismissed, election would be conducted within six months. Local body institutions are not merely to carry out schemes evolved by central and state governments with the resources allocated by the federal and state governments. They have more responsibilities than the assigned and they have to chalk out various programmes based on the local needs peculiar to the local areas with the resources available locally. Their activities are not so rigid. Harnessing the local resources at the optimum level without causing any damage to environment is yet another important function. Yet in the present context to meet the basic minimum needs of the local areas, they need more resources from the state and central governments. To make the local body institutions sound in financial resources to meet the requirements, a State Finance Commission has been constituted to make recommendations. The inherent weakness in the previous panchayati system with regard to finance has been eliminated by this provision through the new act.

People's participation is *sine qua non* for development and it has been realised through the creation of a body at grass-root level called "Gram Sabha". All eligible registered voters are members of Gram Sabha. The Gram Sabha has many functions.

Though it seems that the concept of Gram Sabha is an unworkable proposition in the villages in the present context of caste and communal clashes among communities, somehow or other, it has to be made workable to perform certain specific functions to bring peace, harmony, development and to nurture democracy at the grass-root level. Today there is no institutional devise to train the people in the democratic process so also there is no instrument or device to aggregate the interest or problems of the people. The skill and knowledge of the people have not been harnessed for the development of the society as opportunity has not been provided to the people. People have not been involved in any of the development process from planning to implementation of schemes and programmes. It has created a gap between the government and the people and as a result there is no transparency in the transactions of the government. All those weaknesses will be avoided by involving the people in the development process through Gram Sabha. Gram Sabha will enable the people to share their knowledge with others. It enables the village to have concrete data base for planning. It provides opportunity to the people to express their grievances and demands. It creates avenues to reduce the social tension and that Gram Sabha develops a new democratic culture through its meetings where everybody gets a chance to speak and listen to others. Reservation of seats in all positions at all levels in local body institutions to women is a landmark in the history of women movement in India. 33.3% of reservation of seats to women in local bodies will provide enough opportunity to the women folk to express their long felt needs. The unutilised resources have been put to use for the well-being of the society. Likewise the reservation of seats for SC/ST draws the attention of all. Reservation of seats is in proportion to the population of SC/ST. In Tamil Nadu near about 24% seats have been earmarked for SC/ST in the local bodies. Thus the characteristics mentioned above do not amplify that it is not only an act by itself but it demonstrates that it is a mass movement for peace, prosperity, equity and democracy. Thus the new Panchayati Raj System will have far reaching implications in the life style of the people. It needs proper understanding of the whole system by the people.

Operationalization of the Act

Though the key characteristics of the new Panchayati Raj System are outlined in the 73rd Amendment to the Constitution of India as a framework, the operational part of the new system depends on the act enacted by the state government. The state governments have enacted legislations to give operational dimension to the key principles of the 73rd constitutional amendment. Though the structure is the same, functions vary from state to state as the state governments find it difficult to operationalise the provisions of the 11th Schedule to all the three tiers of the Panchayati Raj System. Attempts are made at different levels to earmark responsibilities to all the three tiers of the Panchayati institutions from the subjects given in the 11th Schedule. District panchayat is only a coordinating agency. It can coordinate and supervise the activities of the middle level panchayats in terms of evolving proposals and implementing programmes and schemes for development. Planning monitoring and evaluation are entrusted to district panchayat. Block or middle level panchayat is entrusted with the responsibility of implementing the schemes and programmes in the whole of the block. Gram Panchayats are entrusted with the responsibility of aggregating the needs and demands of the local populace and plan for the redressal of the needs and grievances of the people. It has to monitor the programmes implemented by the Block Panchayats.

Critical Examination

Logically speaking, more number of development programmes and schemes are to be evolved from below but at present more development schemes and programmes are chalked out at the national level and pushed through the state government to the grass-roots for implementation. Gradually this trend has to vanish. At present one would find more number of overlapping categories of functions allocated to various levels as subjects are such nature that they are to be taken at different levels for different functions and moreover they are the subjects which demand responsibilities on the part of the operators and not of power. Responsibilities can be shared among the institutions without much difficulty. Even today schemes are innumerable for the development of the society but they are not known to the people. Absolutely there is no transparency at the level of the government. Though the new system has got constitutional recognition, it should not conduct itself as a government. It should be a flexible instrument in the hands of the communities.

The people and the leaders should know their responsibilities and duties. They should assess the local resources available at their ends, skills available with the local populace and technology available with them. They should chalk out schemes and programmes based on the untied money allocated to them from the above, money collected from the people as authorised by the authority and the income generated out of the community assets.

Moreover the facilities created in the fifty years for the benefit of the people have to be examined and assessed and appropriate steps should be taken to revamp the facilities already created. Proper maintenance of the institutions under the jurisdiction of the Panchayati bodies will deliver goods. By identifying and harnessing the technology available in the local areas would reduce the load of the problems. Likewise by providing opportunity to make use of the local skills would improve the quality of life in the rural areas. Thus the new system has got more flexibility and this provision enables the leaders to take up more responsibilities to perform the earmarked functions. The new task of the local body leaders is to create awareness among the people about the system and the people should know how the new system could be used for the benefit of the people.

Conclusion

It is not power that matters in Panchayati Raj System. It is the responsibility which makes the system to function effectively. This new arrangement is an approach and a perspective. It is a small government approach which reduces the massive structure of the government and increases the responsibilities of the people. The idea of the modern government that development of the society is the result of the effort of the government, has been changed. Government is not a provider but a facilitator for the people to take initiative to bring development, equity and social justice. To make this system work effectively, the mass has to be conscientised. The people and their representatives should be educated to understand the role and responsibilities of the individual in the new system. By taking up the responsibilities, the individuals can administer development more effectively than the government. The need of the hour is resourcefulness of the people.

Steps to be taken

1. Awareness should be created among the people about the implications of the new system.
2. Training should be given to the elected leaders on their role and responsibilities.
3. Elected leaders should be acquainted with the process of planning from the below.
4. Elected leaders should be equipped with the devices of resource management.
5. Elected leaders should be provided with adequate information on the twenty-nine subjects earmarked for local body institutions.

2

THE NEW PANCHAYATI RAJ SYSTEM IN TAMIL NADU

The new Panchayati Raj System came into being in Tamil Nadu after enacting a new law for local body institutions in the year 1994. Till the arrival of the DMK party to power, it was only an act beyond that local body institutions have not taken any shape in reality. The DMK came to power and it has decided to conduct the election as per its promise to the people given at the time of election and it did conduct the election simultaneously to all the tiers of the rural local bodies along with the urban local bodies. The conduct of election to local bodies has given life to grass-root democracy. Yet the ills attached to the act still continue in the functioning of local bodies.

The salient features of the new act are as follows:

(a) A three-tier system;
(b) Gram Sabha;
(c) Establishment of Election Commission;
(d) Constitution of Finance Commission;
(e) Reservation of seats for SC/ST proportionate to their population;
(f) One-third reservation of seats for women; and
(g) Constitution of District Planning Committee.

Gram Sabha

Gram Sabha is the nucleus of the New Panchayati

Raj System. All the registered voters are the members of the Gram Sabha of that village Panchayat. It has to meet thrice a year and atleast once in six months. President of Gram Panchayat is the presiding officer of the meetings of Gram Sabha. Gram Sabha has to give approval to the budget proposal and annual plan of the village Panchayat. Further it has to give approval to the annual audited statement on the expenditure of the village Panchayat. One-third forms the quorum to transact the business of the Gram Sabha. In Tamil Nadu Gram Sabha is a neglected subject and unit in the local body arrangement as both elected leaders and the officials have not shown any interest in it due to many reasons. As per the Government orders, even beneficiaries for many government schemes are to be selected only in the Gram Sabha. But in reality it does not happen. Beneficiaries are selected not in Gram Sabha but in Panchayat Council which is violative of the provision of the Local Body Act of Tamil Nadu. It is a government approved unconstitutional activity. Government of Tamil Nadu emphasizes the transparent activities in all government's programmes and schemes but there is no way to execute it as Gram Sabha is made defunct. It is a nightmare to many who have been enjoying power and resources all along.

Village Panchayat

A Village Panchayat or Gram Panchayat is constituted for a minimum of five hundred population. Village Panchayat has got members ranging from minimum of five to maximum of fifteen. For Village Panchayat the ward members and the president, are to be elected directly by the voters. Vice-President of the Village Panchavat is elected indirectly among the elected ward members of the Village Panchayat. Village Panchayat has to look after the following subjects:

(a) Construction, repair and maintenance of village panchayat roads;
(b) Lighting of public roads and public places;
(c) Providing drainage facilities;
(d) Cleaning of streets;
(e) Providing public latrines;
(f) Providing burial and burning grounds;
(g) Providing water for washing and bathing purposes; and
(h) Such other duties notified by the Government then and there.

To enable the Village Panchayat to perform its functions, the following decisions have been taken and notified through Government orders:

(a) All Village Panchayats will get financial resources from the Government directly without any intermediary. Panchayati Union or Block Panchayat will not interfere in the process;
(b) Gram Panchayat Presidents have been designated as Executive Heads and they have been entrusted with powers and responsibilities;
(c) Village Panchayat roads can be taken up for works with the resolution of the Panchayats;
(d) Facilities like street light, water supply can be maintained and attended to if there is any disrepair;
(e) Part time clerks can be appointed by the Panchayat president;
(f) House construction plan approval has to be given by the village Panchayats;

(g) Beneficiaries for the central government schemes and programmes have to be selected by the Gram Panchayat in the Gram Sabha;

(h) New Library and information centre in the villages has to be established by the village Panchayat.

Panchayati Union

For each development block a panchayat union is formed. Each panchayati union has a Chair-Person and a Vice-Chairperson elected indirectly by the members of the Panchayat council. Union Council Members are elected directly by the people. For every 5,000 population, one union council member will be elected by the people. Members of Parliament and Legislative Assembly elected from that area are ex-officio members of the panchayat union council.

Panchayati union has the following duties and responsibilities:

(a) Construction, repair and maintenance of Public roads;

(b) Establishment and maintenance of dispensaries;

(c) Construction and maintenance of elementary schools;

(d) Preventive and remedial measures connected with any epidemic;

(e) Conduct of fairs and festivals;

(f) Veterinary relief;

(g) Opening and maintenance of Panchayat Union markets;

(h) Extension of village sites and regulation of buildings;

(i) Maintenance of statistics related to births and deaths;

(j) Improvement of agriculture and agriculture stocks;

(k) Promotion and encouragement of cottage industries;

(l) Other duties and responsibilities entrusted to Panchayati Union by the Government through Government notification.

To enable the panchayat union to perform its duties the Government of Tamil Nadu has issued notification to take up the following activities:

(a) Construction and maintaining Panchayat Union roads, irrigation tanks, and lakes, initiating family welfare activities, executing noon meal schemes and implementing schemes for Adi Dravidas;

(b) Works have to be identified from Employment Assurance schemes and they are to be executed;

(c) Drought relief works have to be identified and executed;

(d) M.P. and M.L.A. area development schemes akin to union have to be executed;

(e) Panchayat union buildings have to be maintained by the union itself;

(f) Panchayat union can supervise the activities in the domain of public health, primary education, drinking water supply, roads, small culverts, khadi and village industries works, technical training education, libraries, rural electricity and non-conventional energy.

Panchayat union administrative arrangement has been modified by which works have been classified into two divisions and entrusted to Block Development Officer and Assistant Block Development Officer. The two sections work independently with their supporting staff. Infrastructural facilities have also been divided and attached to the two divisions.

District Panchayat

District Panchayat is constituted with the directly elected members for every 50,000 population and indirectly elected chair-person and vice-chairperson among the council members. Members of Parliament and State Legislative Assembly of that area are the ex-officio members of the District Panchayat Council. District Panchayat will have to perform the following functions:

(a) Advise the government in all matters concerning Panchayati Raj institutions particularly on services and development programmes;

(b) Watching the progress of the measures undertaken by the government, village Panchayats and Panchayat union councils in the districts as under the administrative control of the districts;

(c) Classification of markets, fairs and public roads in Panchayati Raj institutions; and

(d) Collection of data, publication of statistics, demanding any information from village Panchayats and panchayati union councils.

To enable the district Panchayat to perform the earmarked functions, an administrative change has been effected and by which the Divisional Development Office which is nearer to the district headquarters will supervise the district Panchayat activities. Yet another office which is away from the headquarters will look after auditing of the District

Panchayat activities and the third one will be attached to District Panchayat.

District Planning Committee

Government of Tamil Nadu shall constitute in every district a District Planning Committee to consolidate the plans prepared by the District Panchayat, Panchayat union councils, village Panchayats, municipal councils, and municipal corporations in the district and to prepare a draft development plan for the district as a whole. The committee shall consist of the Collector of the district, members of the House of People who represent whole or part of the district, members of the council of states, Members of Legislative Assembly whose constituencies lie within the district, Mayor of the city municipal corporation and all chair-persons of the municipalities of the district, chair-person of the district Panchayat, one-fifth of the total number of chair-persons of town Panchayats and Panchayati union notified by the government every year by rotation, and such number of persons not less than four-fifth of the total number of the committee as specified by the government elected from among the members of district panchayat, town Panchayats, municipal councils and corporations in the district in proportion to the ratio between the population of the rural areas and of the urban areas. The district Collector is the Chair-person, district Panchayat president is the Vice-Chairperson and chief executive officer of the district Panchayat is the secretary of the district planning committee. The Committee shall allocate funds to various schemes to the Panchayats and Panchayat union and shall monitor the implementation of these schemes.

Reservation

One-third of positions at all levels of the bodies are reserved for women. SC and ST get reservation of positions at all levels of the bodies in proportion to their population.

Election and Finance Commissions

An Election Commission headed by the State Election Commissioner appointed by the Governor to conduct the local body elections is mandatory. The election commissioner enjoys powers and privileges and status of a judge of the High Court. The tenure of office of the Election Commissioner is two years. However, the Commissioner can be given extension for four more years.

There will be a Finance Commission constituted every fifth year to review financial positions of the Panchayats and to make recommendations to the Governor as to fix the principles to govern the distribution between the state and Panchayats of the net proceeds of the taxes, duties, tolls and fees leviable by the Government which may be divided between them and allocation between the district Panchayats, Panchayat union councils and village Panchayats of their respective shares of such proceeds. Further to identify the logistics for making grants in aid to the panchayats from the consolidated fund of the state and the measures needed to improve the financial position of the panchayats. The Finance Commission shall consist of a chairman and four other members.

Critical Evaluation

The present act does not provide much scope for giving life to the spirit of the 73rd Constitutional

Amendment Act in the Tamil Nadu Panchayat Act of 1994. Subjects in the 11th Schedule do not find a place in the body of the act especially in the chapter on functions of Panchayat bodies. Development officials who work in the Panchayat bodies are declared as government officials and they do not come under the purview of local bodies. As a result, the local bodies cannot supervise the activities of the officials of the local bodies. While comparing the old Act of Panchayati Raj of 1958 with the new one, one would find adequate powers had been given to local bodies in the old act to supervise, regulate and control the officials working in the local bodies. District Collector is vested with the power of controlling the village Panchayats. District Collector's arbitrary power to suspend and dissolve the Gram Panchayats is against the spirit of decentralization of powers. DRDA (District Rural Development Agency) is a registered body, which is under the control of the project officer and the District Collector. It is a *kamadhenu* where all centrally and state sponsored programmes have been pooled and distributed. It is yet another factor hampering the functioning of the local bodies. When new Panchayati Raj System began to function, the centrally sponsored and state sponsored schemes and programmes have to be reduced and instead more new schemes have been introduced at present by the Governments. In Tamil Nadu two schemes such as Anna Marumalarchi Thittam (Anna Renaissance Scheme) and Namakku Name Schemes (we for our-selves) have been launched. Yet another scheme namely MP's and MLA's Area Development schemes work against the interest of local bodies.

Gram Sabha has not yet been activated to develop democratic culture in decision making, to bring transparency in the activities of the government and to involve the people in the development process of the community. Enactment of legislation and conduct of election alone will not bring any change in the functioning of the local bodies. Proper enhancement of the capacity of the leaders, enabling suitable government orders and provision of adequate resources can alone bring needed change in the functioning of the local bodies.

Aftermath of Election

Election to rural and urban local bodies has been conducted and elected leaders assumed responsibilities. After the election, resources to the tune of rupees one crore to each District Panchayats, rupees ten lakhs to every Panchayat union and rupees seventy crores to the Gram Panchayat of the state have been allocated. The amount has been spent by the respective institutions as per the specification given by the State Government. Yet the basic problems are not met. On 29th November, 1996 the State Finance Commission has submitted its report to the Government of Tamil Nadu. The demand for more powers has increased from the elected leaders of local bodies irrespective of the party affiliation and this has compelled the State Government to convene the meeting of the leaders of local bodies by the Chief Minister of Tamil Nadu on 30th November and 1st December 1997. He assured the representatives that steps will be taken to devolve powers and to increase the financial resources to local bodies. In the meanwhile Tamil Nadu Forest Department has decided to hand over 3.5 lakh hectares of social forest lands to the local bodies. In the month of January 1997 Panchayat union chair-persons have been given a three-day training. In March 1997 while presenting the budget the Chief Minister emphasized the fact that elected leaders would be given adequate powers to take decisions and execute programmes and schemes. 8% of share will be given to local bodies from the tax pool declared by the Government. Thus the Government of Tamil Nadu has increased the allocation from Rs. 646 crores to Rs. 1174 crores. But it does not meet the requirements of the local bodies.

Local body leaders have formed associations to represent their problems. Following the demands of the representatives of the people, announcements have been made with regard to provision of sitting fee and travelling allowances to the local body leaders. L.C. Jain committee which was constituted after the election to work out details to devolve powers, has submitted its preliminary report and based on it a Government order was issued which carries the details of the powers and responsibilities of the three tiers of rural local body. L.C. Jain has submitted the final report of the committee to the Government of Tamil Nadu.

Government of Tamil Nadu has issued an order by which it made the District Collector as the chair-person of the District Planning Committee. L.C. Jain, Tamil Nadu Planning Commission member tendered his resignation to protest against the decision of the Government of Tamil Nadu making district collector as the president of District Planning Committee. This has sensitised the leaders of this province. Union Finance Minister P. Chidambaram and opposition leader in the State Legislative Assembly S. Balakrishnan repeatedly criticised the Government of Tamil Nadu for its procrastination in devolving powers and resources to local bodies.

In the meanwhile Government of Tamil Nadu pleaded with the Central Government to bring an amendment to the 73rd constitutional amendment to enable the state to have two-tier structure for

Government of Tamil Nadu. To satisfy the demands of the political parties a committee has been constituted by inviting representatives from various political parties to suggest ways and means to devolve powers to local bodies. Political parties which do not share power in the Assembly have started exerting pressure on the state government to devolve powers to local bodies.

It is true that there are very many weaknesses in the act itself and a variety of existing acts do not permit the state to devolve powers. The capacity of the leaders are not so high to handle all the subjects earmarked for Panchayati Raj and yet leaders are alert and optimistic at present that Panchayat System is the only solution to solve most of the problems in the rural areas. Steps are on to rectify the defects. Local body leaders are putting a one point demand to the state government to devolve adequate powers and resources to the local bodies. Expected pressure has come from the people for devolution of powers and the leaders of local bodies have come to a stage to take powers from the state government on their own in the event of denial of powers to the local bodies.

3

GRASS-ROOT DEMOCRACY YET TO START IN TAMIL NADU

Introduction

Even today people quote the Uthiramerur inscription to portray that Tamil society has its own rich tradition of keeping Panchayat as system of self governing institution with the characteristics of liberal democracy. It is not only for political meetings and academic discussions but in reality Panchayat has been viewed as an anathema and unwanted demon to the present system of governance as it would be detrimental to the existing arrangement of brokerage contact politics. But the mandated provisions of the 73rd and 74th constitutional amendment acts have been compelling the state government to initiate certain actions to meet the constitutional obligations of conducting election to local bodies, constituting high level committee to devolve powers to three tiers of local bodies and allocating more financial resources to local bodies. These are some of the concomitant steps taken by the state government to fulfil the constitutional obligations. Yet the problems of the new system are multidimensional which need the attention of the state and federal government immediately.

The Problem

The events such as murdering the *dalit* president of the Melavalavu Gram Panchayats, supplying thirty-seven rules books, and three Bank Account books along with cheque books to the president of Gram Panchayat, asking the Gram Panchayat presidents to prepare proposal to get financial sanction to provide facilities, exerting pressure on the president of Gram Panchayats by the MLAs, MPs and Ministers to select beneficiaries to utilise the fund, keeping the functionaries working in the panchayati system accountable to the government and not to the Panchayats, giving one crore rupees to each MP and twenty-five lakhs of rupees to each MLA for rural development activities, proliferating more number of sponsored schemes (both Centre and State) to the local bodies without making them to plan for financial resources from the government without providing adequate opportunities to mobilize resources on their own, creating a structure of three tiers in such a manner to generate conflict among the three tiers and not allowing the local bodies to have control over local resources will bring a plethora of problems to destabilise the new Panchayati Raj System.

Status of Tamil Nadu Panchayat

The drawbacks which we found in the functioning of the local bodies in Tamil Nadu due to the act, are not the designed move of the present Government under the leadership of M. Karunanidhi. The defective act was prepared and presented in the Legislative Assembly in a hurry and hasty manner and it was approved by the members of the AIADMK under the leadership of J. Jeyalalitha. The new act has been carefully scrutinized and evaluated in many fora by the leaders and intellectuals and they have indicated the loopholes in it. Yet there was no systematic political pressure to the then Government to implement the act by conducting the election to the local bodies. In the meanwhile to escape from the constitutional obligation, it was alleged that the then Government took shelter under the court case filed by someone who questioned the logic of reservation of seats in the local bodies for backward classes. Only a few NGOs and Gandhian institutions have consistently worked for awareness creation among the rural populace about the new Panchayati Raj System.

The Eleventh general election has drawn the attention of the political parties towards the new Panchayati Raj system. Dravida Munnetra Kazhagam had prominently highlighted the failure of the AIADMK in conducting the election to local bodies and it promised the people in its manifesto that it would conduct the election to local bodies immediately if it returns to power. After it came to power, at a stroke it conducted the election to the local bodies both urban and rural after issuing an ordinance of withdrawing the provision to reserve seats to backward class in the local bodies. Certain changes have been introduced in the system of Tamil Nadu local bodies by the DMK Government before the conduct of the election. Gram Panchayat has been freed from the clutches of the political parties, and the provision of one-fifth of representatives drawing from Gram Panchayats to Block Panchayats, from Block Panchayats to District Panchayats has been withdrawn.

After the election, the elected representatives to local bodies from varied strata of the society with high hopes and aspirations went into the portrals of power. During the electioneering the media has highlighted the important implications of local bodies and the increasing monetary flow to local bodies which probably drew the attention of all sections to participate in the electoral process. As electioneering process demanded money, candidates who have contested the election had to spend money. Thus the candidates have spent the money with the hope that they can take it back from the schemes that are going to be implemented through their respective bodies and the beneficiaries. Post election scenario has projected a dismal picture about the activities of the leaders as the officials went on carrying out their works unmindful of the elected leaders who have been in office. The officials without having any guidance from the State Government acted in a manner suitable to their advantage by using the provisions available in the old act and tried their level best to involve the elected leaders in the contract system to perform certain development works sponsored by both state and central governments.

In the meanwhile the cry for powers has been vociferous and as a result a meeting of local body leaders was convened by the Chief Minister immediately after the election and the elected leaders were asked to express their difficulties. In fact the leaders expalined their position that they have no power and resources and they are not respected by the officials and their words have not been given due respect in the offices and of course they demanded certain facilities to them as the local body leaders enjoy elsewhere. Finally the Chief Minister delivered his speech with a pessimistic note. Yet the cry for power has not come to an end and instead it has increased. The local body leaders formed associations and discussed their problems and sent their resolutions to the Government.

Moreover union Finance Minister P. Chidamabaram and the opposition leader in State Legislative Assembly S. Balakrishnan have joined issue with the Chief Minister on the procrastination of the state government in devolving powers and resources to the local bodies. People's expectations from the leaders of local bodies have increased and hence the representatives of the local bodies have been pressurised by the people for services and facilities to the people. Having understood the restlessness of the local body leaders, the Government of Tamil Nadu has appointed a committee under the Chairmanship of L.C. Jain to work out the modalities of transferring power and resources to local bodies. The committee has submitted an interim report to enable the government to devolve powers so as to make the panchayats take up works for providing facilities and services to the people. Before passing the recommendations and issuing G.O. the leaders have been made to fight against each other by making use of the loopholes in the arrangement of the structure.

The very purpose of constituting this arrangement is to make each unit as an autonomous body to tackle certain problems depending on their capacity. But in reality each tier is working against another due to duplication of work and duality of the roles. The Gram Panchayat has its own jurisdiction of work. But the Block Panchayat ward members hailing from the same place claim that they are equivalent to that of the Gram Panchayat President and hence they demand certain specific powers at par with the president. On the same basis Zilla Parishad members also claim the same. They demand powers equivalent to the presidents of Block Panchayats.

In reality nobody knows which body has what powers? Acts, decisions and policies are put into practice only through Government orders. Government officials have not received any order from the Government of Tamil Nadu till October 1996. Restlessness of the leaders of local bodies has increased the tension and it compelled the state authorities to take initiative to devolve powers. The state government exerted pressure on the Planning Commission and especially on L.C. Jain to submit his interim report and thereby an interim report was submitted. In the meanwhile the elected leaders have been asked to undergo one day training conducted by the officials. Dos and donts have been read in the programme and it had not invoked any interest among the leaders. Finally in the month of October 1996, an order was issued by the Government of Tamil Nadu.

The G.O. issued by the Government has taken near about four months to reach the Gram Panchayat Presidents. Even in the G.O. the Government has not stated any original function for the Panchayats. It has mentioned only agency functions.

Implementing schemes of the federal government is mentioned as powers of the Panchayats. After issuing the Government order the presidents of Gram Panchayats have been changed as contractors. Beneficiaries to schemes have to be selected by the Gram Sabha. When this is the practice, as per the provision of the act the ward members of Panchayati union demanded such role for them. The schemes allotted to Block Panchayat have been distributed among the members. Likewise the Zilla Panchayat members demanded such powers to carry out certain works in the schemes sponsored by the Central Government. Thus the elected representatives of local bodies have developed a perception that they have to carry out the programmes and schemes of the federal and state government without knowing the original functions of the local body institutions.

It is interesting to note that the representatives of the people in the local bodies have imbibed the qualities of the MLAs and MPs and have been acting in the same way as MLAs and MPs are behaving and performing in their respective constituencies. MPs are working in the local bodies through their local Area Development scheme with an amount of one crore rupees and MLAs are working in the local bodies through their scheme with an amount of twenty-five lakh rupees for a year. These have reduced the importance of the representatives of the local bodies. Since local body institutions have enormous amount of money to be spent, interferences of the representatives are frequent and intense.

The local body leaders do not know the background of the 73rd amendment to the Constitution of India, main provisions of the amendment, key provisions of the State act, major schemes of both the federal and provincial government, availability of resources, and process of micro level planning as they have been inferred from a variety of need assessment studies. As candidates contesting for Assembly and Parliament election, the candidates have contested in the local body election. After the election, the elected representatives without knowing the full implications of the local bodies started functioning as liaison between the people and the officials. They consider local body institutions as political institutions instead of development institutions.

The Government also slowly has enabled the elected representatives to enjoy the comforts of MLAs and MPs. Before giving any clear cut powers and responsibility, the state government has provided one Ambassador car to the President of the Zilla Panchayat. He has been provided with a good office in the collectorate without any power to take decision in the functioning of the development institutions in the collectorate such as district rural development agency. Likewise Tata Sumo a luxury van has been provided to every Block Panchayat which is being used by the Panchayati union chair-person, perks have been announced to the local body leaders. Sitting fees and travel concessions have been fixed with ceiling.

While the representatives of the people have been in full swing in sharing the responsibility of executing the schemes and programmes of the state and centre governments, Government of Tamil Nadu has issued an ordinance making district collector as chair-person of District Planning Committee. To protest against this decision, L.C. Jain member of the State Planning Commission tendered his resignation. This has sensitised the leaders of various political parties and they demanded that District Panchayat president should be made the chair-person of the District Planning Committee. Still this controversy has not been resolved. As a result of intensive criticism the Government of Tamil Nadu has come out with a decision to constitute another Committee of representatives of all political parties to go into the details of the problems akin to devaluation of power. So far the committee has not started functioning.

Inferences

DMK is a ruling party in the province of Tamil Nadu. In the local bodies DMK has gained major portion of seats along with TMC. Yet there is reluctance on the part of the leaders to devolve powers to local bodies. This unwillingness to part with power to local body leaders by the State Government has created a lurking fear among the local body leaders that the Panchayati institutions will be disturbed covertly and overtly.

The local body leaders have an orientation of Politics rather than an orientation of Development. They have started doing agency functions without knowing their original functions. Contractors are replaced by the elected leaders, without proper capacity building exercise and hence the local body leaders find it difficult to perform their role. There is no scope for micro level planning in the present arrangement of devolution of powers.

The local bodies have no control over the resources. Their share in the resource mobilization is very limited. Dissemination of information is very rare among the leaders. MPs and MLAs schemes have limited the scope of local body leaders activities in the rural areas. There is inadequate intellectual input to the local body institutions. The officials who are performing the role mentioned in the subjects earmarked for Panchayati Raj institutions, are reluctant to come under the jurisdiction of the local bodies due to the lukewarm attitude of the state level leaders and the government. Thus, the Panchayati Raj in Tamil Nadu is not an institution of self governance.

Conclusion

Local body institutions are at the mercy of the state government for their functioning with powers and adequate resources. The very logic of decentralization of power is lost sight of. From the available perception it is inferred that local bodies are viewed as agents to carry out the schemes and programmes of the governments. The poor capacity and political perception of the grass-root level leaders have intensified the state leaders perception that the sudden devolution of powers would decentralise corruption.

These issues have to be tackled expeditiously and for which political support base has to be created to devolve powers to local bodies in the absence of political will on the part of the leaders at the state level. The existing laws which are deterrent to the main provision of the Panchayati Raj Act are to be modified. The institutional mechanism to empower the leaders to manage the institutions must be developed which will be the only option available at present.

4

GRASS-ROOT LEADERS' PERCEPTION OF POWERS

Introduction

Elections to local bodies have given a new impetus for the functioning of development institutions at the grass-root level. Yet, confusion and confrontation among the members' role and function, power and authority, and work and responsibilities continue to haunt the minds of the elected leaders for the past nine months. The concept of devolution of power not only brought jittery among the officials who have enjoyed enormous powers in the absence of elected bodies, but also the members of legislative assembly and members of parliament as it involves lakhs of elected representatives in the decision making process. Moreover, the representatives of the people to the State Legislature and National Paliament will have more political orientation than development orientation, as they have been deeply involved in political activities for a long period rather than in development activities.

National Parliament and State Legislatures are policy making bodies which have more support base from top level bureaucracy. But local body institutions are not only taking decisions but also executing the same in the field. The representatives of the local bodies will have more responsibilities in terms of constituency service than the members of legislature and national parliament. The area of operation of local body leaders is also limited in terms of space. For the success of the local body institutions, the development perception and orientation of representatives are essential as the role and function of local body demand development work. Hence, it is imperative that the local body leaders should have development orientation apart from political orientation. Members of Legislature and Parliament can get re-elected even without contributing anything for a period of five years, as their job is to aggregate the demands of the people and articulate the same in the authoritative bodies for decision making. Further, their success is always linked with their party's performance and image whereas the local body leaders' success in the election depends on how they work in their constituencies. It is linked with the performance of the leaders. Against this background, it is felt that the local body leaders should have development orientation and development perception.

The Problem

Leaders of local bodies, ever since their election, continue their demand for more powers to them for taking initiative to development work in their constituencies. They further posited that the state and the federal government have to provide enough fund to meet the requirements of the people with the belief that the local body leaders are to execute the government schemes and programmes with the fund allocated to the schemes. They further believe that give away' dolls is the primary function of the elected representatives of the local bodies. Whereas the members of State Legislature and National Parliament demanded certain amount of money to carry out certain works relating to rural development, though they have other functions. The present context posited a diffused situation in which the representatives of the people from the village ward members to members of parliament have been confronting with each other in allocation of powers and responsibilities even though powers and responsibilities are earmarked specifically as they have role ambiguity and role conflict. It is imperative that the local body leaders should have development perception since they have to carry out development activities. The question is whether they have development perception to perceive the new system in right perspective.

Theoretical Perspective

Literature on representative process is abundant and adequate and yet the distinctions between the representative roles of the provincial legislators and the national parliament are not adequately explored. Typologies and frameworks have been developed to explain various aspects of the representative institutions of the developed nations. But there is dearth of literature on the representative process of the local body institutions. The local body institutions have not been considered seriously by the scholars as representative institutions. There are reasons for this stand. The local body institutions are not decisions making bodies but they are only implementing agencies. In most of the countries local body institutions are to implement the federal and state governments' programmes and schemes.

Success of the representative institutions fully relied on the proper understanding of the representatives about their own role and function. There are several roles to be performed by members of Legislative Assembly and National Parliament in a given context. They may vary from period to period and society to society. It is a mutual relationship between the representatives and the constituents. Constituents' perception of representation could also be counted for the functioning of the representative democracy. In India, there are three levels of representative institutions namely national parliament, state legislatures and local body institutions. People use to project collective and individual demands to the members of parliament and legislature on most of the occasions they are called recommendations. The assignments are not mandatory and they are recommendatory. But the local body institutions are meant for providing service facilities and development activities. Moreover, the proximity between the representatives of the people in the local bodies and the people is so close. People's claim over the local body leaders is intensive and likewise their expectations and demands are heavy and more than what they expect from members of legislature and parliament. To fulfil the demands, expectations and aspirations of the people, the local body leaders should have enough capacity, power and authority with adequate financial resources.

To identify the resourcefulness of the local body leaders, an attempt is made here. It is a part of the programme by which the leaders have been invited for a training programme. Before peeping into the programme, the representatives have been requested to give their feedback about their perception, and vision of the new system and their achievements.

Methodology

Representatives have not been given any prepared schedule or document. They have been grouped into four divisions and they have been asked to prepare a report about the implications of the new system, their perception, people's demands, available resources and their managerial ability. First category of groups represent the Dharmapuri and Dindigul district panchayat members. Second category of groups represent the Erode district gram panchayat leaders. Total number of respondents participated in the programme come to one hundred and sixty. One hundred and twenty from Gram Panchayats and forty from District Panchayats. Their reactions are categorised into many divisions based on the issues. Their reactions will be discussed in the following pages.

73rd Amendment

It is a pity to note that none of them are aware of the key characteristics of the 73rd constitutional amendment. No one has a copy of the amendment and nobody bothered about it, nor participated in any of the awareness programmes. They became representatives because the party has selected them to contest for positions in the local bodies with the hope that they can get adequate resources to be distributed among the people through schemes. Since everybody talked much about the new system, they believed that they can also get their shares and do service for the people. During interaction, they said that they never had a glance of the 73rd Constitutional Amendment Act even after they became representatives of the people in the local bodies. They continue to harp on the subjects namely water supply, rural roads, sanitation, street light and IRDP as the powers of local bodies. 243(G) in the act emphasises the fundamentals of the amendment act. It says that the new system of government is to bring economic development and social justice. In the discussion, it was elaborated by referring events from the activities of the federal government.

While listening to the observation of the members one would notice the fact that the representatives of the people in the local bodies from Gram Panchayat to district panchayat are not aware of the key provisions of the 73rd constitutional amendment act, and representatives have embarked in the functioning of local body institutions and for which they rely on the official who work in the respective levels of offices. When the officials came to know that the newly elected representatives of the people to the local bodies have no grip over the powers and functions of the new system, they continue to dominate in the system of keeping them in the dark.

Tamil Nadu Panchayati Act 1994

Tamil Nadu rural local body act of 1994 is a bulky volume in archaic Tamil and legalistic English. Common man cannot read either English or Tamil version of the act. Further the act has been operationalised through the rules framed by the bureaucracy. Both the act and rules are dry and people would find it very difficult to understand. Of course, to circumvent these difficulties, there are a few institutions which have brought out simplified version of the act with notes and explanations. The organisations are Gandhigram Rural Institute, CHERU, Dindigul, Legal Resources for Social Action, Satyamurthy Centre for Democratic Studies, Shanti Ashram and a few other NGOs. The representatives have neither gone through the government documents nor the documents prepared by the NGOs. After getting into the local bodies through election they are blinking without knowing full details of the act and implications of the new system of governance.

Training to Local Body Leaders

After the election to local bodies, Government of Tamil Nadu have decided to organise a crash training programme for the elected leaders. One day training programme was organised for local body leaders throughout Tamil Nadu and do's and don'ts have been imparted to the leaders by the officials. It was a mere reading session where the officials have read the documents to the leaders. The leaders could not make out anything from the training. The elected leaders are having varied capacities. One would find illiterate to post-graduate degree holder occupying positions in local bodies. Training is a continuous programme. It could be given in several phases. More practical inputs should be given for the local body leaders. Field oriented training is an imperative need of the hour for rural local body leaders. From micro level plan to common resources management, a leader has to be equipped in many areas of activities. There are different levels in the local bodies namely Gram Panchayats, Panchayat Union and District Panchayat. At every level, the role and responsibilities have to be defined. Since the act is a defective one in Tamil Nadu, series of attempts have to be made to define and redefine the role and responsibilities of the three tiers of the local body institutions. This process took several months to complete. From October 1996, the Government of Tamil Nadu has started issuing Government orders with regard to devolution of powers. Even before issuing government orders, Government of Tamil Nadu allocated money for rural development activities. To spend the earmarked money at appropriate level, officials have consulted the elected representatives. The elected representatives thought that the discretion they have enjoyed in utilising the money is the power of the elected representatives. Hence, they talk much about resources and their power to utilise the resources. Those who do not get such discretionary powers, have started posing demand for powers. Thus, misunderstanding among the representatives has grown to the level of passing resolution in the bodies against each other and conflicts are arising between village Panchayati presidents and Panchayati Union council members, Panchayati Union chair-person and District Panchayati councillors. Till Panchayat presidents were given powers, Panchayati Union councillors, along with their chair-person, carried out the activities of the union without consulting Panchayat presidents. They feel that the village Panchayati presidents are unwanted elements. After issuing G.O. No. 226, Panchayati union councillors have been made not to use the power of Gram Panchayati presidents. District Panchayati councillors and the presidents thought that they would get powers like powers of district collector. It is unfortunate that they cannot do anything even to the level of village Panchayat presidents. They have spent several lakhs of rupees in the election. Now the Government of Tamil Nadu, through its G.O., declared that it is only a coordinating agency.

Village Panchayati Presidents

After the Panchayati election, the presidents believed that they can fulfil the promise they have given to the people at the time of election. It is unfortunate that the presidents could do nothing in the villages and all activities were carried out in the rural areas by the Panchayati union with the help of its staff and contractor. Moreover, the Block Development officers also did not know that powers could be given to the Panchayat presidents in the absence of a government order. Panchayat union chairman and councillors have exerted pressure on the officials to consider certain schemes and programmes recommended by the councillors and chair-person. The officials have considered the recommendations given by the councillors and the chair-persons wherever possible. Village Panchayat presidents also exerted pressure on the officials of the Panchayati union to get share of powers as that of Panchayat union councillors. The officials have given some works in the schemes to the presidents for execution and by which presidents were made as contractors. There are presidents who are satisfied with the contract work given to them by the union. But a major section of the village Panchayati presidents wanted to get the due share of powers to look after the affairs of the villages. The village Panchayati presidents had to face a number of problems as people meet them frequently for better facilities as per their promises. To avoid confrontation among the presidents and Panchayati union councillors, a government order was issued with an objective of handing over some responsibilities to them especially poverty alleviation schemes. Even after issuing the G.O., the presidents were not clear about the procedures. They categorically demand certain schemes for implementation. Even in some of the Panchayati union council meetings, resolutions have been passed in this regard and they made it clear in the councils that the village Panchayati presidents should not enter into the premises of the Panchayati union office. Beyond the poverty alleviation schemes, they were not able to move and comprehend their activities. Their demand lies in sharing the resources earmarked for union activities, among themselves. They demanded certain facilities like phone, office and other paraphernalia for each and every councillor. By their perception and activities, villages are represented by two presidents. It is almost a two-member unit. Since they have been nominated by the political parties, their activities are almost synonymous with Members of Legislative Assembly or Members of Parliament. They are oriented to give recommendation letter to individuals to receive benefits from the schemes of the government. Their activities are more politically oriented than development oriented.

District Panchayati Councillors

District councillors including their president in the event of election thought that the whole district schemes and programmes would be handed over to them. With this brief, they have spent few lakhs of rupees in the election as an investment. They went into the office of the District Panchayat in the collectorate. To their surprise, there is no such establishment excepting a name board near the office of the DRDA. Immediately after the election, a big room has been allotted to the president and provided furnitures to accommodate all the members in the room. People from their respective constituencies gave petitions to the councillors and all of them have been sent to various sections of the Collectorate through the president of the District Panchayat. In the beginning, even the officials have not known what powers the District Panchayats have in the present context. District collectors have been acting as usual without considering the presence of the elected bodies. After a few months, even the petitions submitted by the district councillors have not been considered seriously by the officials. The Government of Tamil Nadu, after receiving pressures from various sections, pronounced its decisions through the Government orders along with allocation of money. It is stated in the Government orders that the District Panchayat has a supervisory role and the earmarked money has to be spent for the establishment of District Panchayats. District administration has spent thirty to forty per cent of the money for the purchase of vehicle and to provide furnitures to the District Panchayat office. It was also decided that the balance money has to be spent for scheme activities. To share the amount for schemes, the councillors have given recommendations. But it is a pity that the schemes recommended by the district councillors have been already recommended by MLA and MP in their area development scheme. Hence, the district councillors do not know what to do in the District Panchayat without having decision making power. They feel that they should have money for schemes as MLA and MP. They further felt that they should be given some perks like phone, free bus pass and few others. They feel that MLAs and MPs are much against devolution of powers to the local bodies.

Another major area which irritated the councillors is the DRDA. The members are not aware that it is an agency registered under Societies Act. They want to have control over DRDA since the activities of DRDA are related to rural development. Further, they do not know the position of the federal government over the DRDA. Now they demand DRDA to be under the control of the District Panchayats.

District Panchayat council has a major role in planning. Mirco level planning assumed significance from Ninth Plan itself. The importance of micro level planning has not been felt by the members of District Panchayats simply because of the fact that they do not realise the value of bottom-up planning. They are not aware of the whole planning exercise. Further, they do not know the new Government order constituting district planning committee. Normally the representatives should have adequate information about the constituency and its requirements. The representatives are not aware of the schemes and programmes of the government towards rural development. All the district councillors are doing their party work in the District Panchayat office by using the phone. They use to receive petition from the people and distribute the same to the various offices. All the representatives from Panchayati union council to district Panchayati president have more political orientation than development orientation.

From the observation of the representatives of the people to the local bodies, one would notice the state of affairs. The representatives have no development orientation. They are not aware of the full implications of the decentralization of power. They neither know the provisions of the new Panchayati act of Tamil Nadu nor the government orders realising the provisions of the new act. They are very particular that the schemes and programmes are to be shared among the representatives of the local bodies. But they do not know the full details of the schemes and programmes. They also demand perks for local body leaders. Thus, the local body leaders have not equipped themselves to handle the powers assigned to them even though powers have been devolved to them. The need of the hour is capacity building on the part of the leaders in local body institutions. Government of Tamil Nadu is not serious about the capacity building of the leaders. The local body leaders felt that the spending of earmarked money for the schemes of rural development is the role and responsibility of local body leaders. They are not making any effort to know the development issues.

5

WOMEN LEADERS' PERCEPTION OF LOCAL BODIES

Introduction

Reservation of seats in the Local Body institutions for the women in all positions as per the provisions of 73rd and 74th Amendment to the Constitution of India, no doubt, is going to create a metamorphosis in the activities of women in polity, economy and society in the years to come. The initial apprehension and doubts over the readiness of women folk to come into power-centres and to take up responsibilities of administering development on their own, have been dispelled by their participation in the electoral process of the local body institutions in the month of October 1996.

The elected leaders of the local bodies in Tamil Nadu have started functioning in their respective domain. While discharging their duties they found problems due to various reasons. Of them lack of training is more visible when compared with other problems, they face. The rule of the game should be taught to them in order to make the elected leaders to handle the office carefully and effectively so as to deliver goods properly to the people. Against this background an administrative training was conceived and carried out throughout the state. But it does not stop with teaching rules and regulations relating to the functioning of the local body institutions. The effective functioning of the leaders fully relies on the leadership qualities of elected representatives. The elected women representatives who have stepped into the portals of power need leadership training essentially. Hence a programme was conceived to offer leadership training to the elected women of urban local bodies.

Designing of the Course

To design the training course, to prepare the course material and to train the resource persons, three meetings were held in Tamil Nadu Institute of Urban Studies, Coimbatore by involving the three agencies (Gandhigram Rural Institute, Avinashilingam Institute for Home Science and Satyamurthy Centre for Democratic Studies) which are selected for offering training to the leaders. The three institutions have shared the responsibilities in contributing to the preparation of the training manual. The Gandhigram Rural Institute has helped the Tamil Nadu Institute of Urban Studies to evolve a common course. Instructions have been given to all the three training institutions about the content to be offered during the training programme. After evolving a common programme the three institutions have embarked in the training programme in their respective areas.

Assistant Directors of Town Panchayats and Regional Directors of Municipal Administration in the respective areas have taken the responsibilities of arranging the programme of training in areas which come under their jurisdiction. Faculty members and resource persons used to take classes for the elected women representatives. Though it is a one day programme, the content of the programme is a well set package. From 10.00 a.m. to 5.00 p.m. with a lunch break of one hour is not enough to carry out the package. Yet it has been carried out with great difficulty.

Training Content

The training programme has the following course content: a detailed discussion on the background of the 74th Constitutional Amendment Act, the salient feature of 74th Amendment Act, and the role of women in administering development in their areas, in utilising the powers conferred on them through the 12th Schedule.

Emphasis was given more on the responsibilities of the leaders than on powers. Further a detailed explanation was offered to distinguish executive and legislative functions of the institutions. The conventional belief of the people that the local bodies are to provide facilities has been changed by emphasising the new responsibility of achieving growth, development, social justice and equity apart from providing the facilities. Further it was explained that the role of the government has been changed. Government is going to be a facilitator not a provider. Community has more responsibilities and thereby state is reducing its powers and size. Thus local body institutions assume greater responsibilities. A few of the modern management techniques have been explained to them. More specifically, explanations have been offered to the elected leaders that how they could work for economic growth and development rather than in building infrastructure facilities alone. The stress was on the small government approach and people's responsibilities. It was also stressed in the training how people could be trained in citizenry in the ward meetings. Further illustrations were given to inculcate democratic spirit and culture in the minds of the people at the grass-root level. While indicating all the powers mentioned in the Act, one would feel that more responsibilities have been given to local bodies beyond their capacity. Further, it was emphasised that capacity of the women leaders should be enhanced to meet the challenges with they face every day in the local areas.

Visuals have been projected through overhead projector about the challenges the women leaders have to face at present while discharging their duties. Solutions have also been offered to all those challenges. Likewise, the available urban development schemes have been explained to them with all details, by quoting the sources for their references. Adequate care was taken to operationalise the powers given to the urban local bodies through the 12th Schedule. The trainees have been asked to note questions while listening to the lectures and they have been requested to pose their questions in the discussion session which started usually by 3.30 P.M. It went upto 5.00 P.M.

After giving all the above information the representatives have expressed their observations.

Participants' Observation

1. No doubt it is a confidence building exercise.
2. After listening to the lectures, we as women look at issues more deeply and critically. Our common sense approach has died and gone.
3. After this leadership training we are conscious of our leadership rather than gender. This programme gave us training how to look at issues as leaders not as women.
4. The mind set of the women leaders that we are to represent women's issues has been changed.

Now we feel that we are only representatives of the people.

5. We came to know the women's issues more deeply only after this programme.
6. We have realised the importance of the reservation of seats for women in local bodies only after listening to the lecture on "Why reservation for women in local bodies?"
7. So far we talked much about the powers to be devolved but after this programme we felt the onerous responsibilities of the elected leaders in administering development.
8. After attending this programme we feel that our capacity today will not be enough to meet the challenges and it should be enhanced.
9. This programme has cleared our doubt as to whether the elected leaders can assume executive functions.
10. Now we started realising the need of harmony between the elected leaders and functionaries for successful functioning of local bodies to meet the aspirations of the people.
11. After listening to the lectures in the programme we came to know the bundle of programmes for the development of the poor. So far we were in the dark.
12. After this programme we have realised the gap between the perception of the government and the people on efforts of development.
13. This programme educated us about the importance of resource mobilization on our own to manage our local affairs without depending much on the fund from the state and central government for the sustainability of the local body institutions.
14. This programme has opened our eyes to look at the opportunities provided by the government to

mobilise the resources locally.

15. We have realised the importance of communication skill for our success.
16. The present fund position should be improved to meet the aspirations of the people.
17. We came to know that for social development of the local areas more than funds, leaders skill and work are essential.
18. This programme has educated the leaders as to how the leaders have to educate the people about their role and responsibilities in the community.
19. This programme has educated us as to how to inculcate the democratic spirit in the minds of the people through conducting meeting of the bodies.

We need more details on the following

1. All the schemes for urban development should be in the published form.
2. We should know how to conduct women's entrepreneurship programme.
3. We need more input on micro level planning.
4. We need more flexibility in administrative procedures.
5. We feel that more schemes have to be evolved area specifically rather than receiving them from the above.
6. We need orientation to the officials as they are in a different mind set that the officials know everything and people's representatives should be educated and trained by the officials.
7. We need some honorarium for our work. Otherwise people will involve in corruption or only the affluent section can alone come forward to serve the people through local body institutions.

8. We need more information on the self employment and entrepreneurship opportunities for women.
9. We need information to build women sangam and Cooperatives.
10. We need training once in six months.
11. We need more models.
12. We need more success field visits.
13. We need regular information dissemination through a newsletter or magazine.

The Pressing Problems in their hands

1. Corruption still prevails.
2. Irregularities in public distribution system.
3. Drinking water facility.
4. Garbage clearance.
5. Sanitation.
6. Negative attitude of the officials.
7. Repairing of roads.
8. Encroachment of the commons by private individuals.
9. Paucity of funds.

Training Setting

Programme should not be for the sake of programme and reporting. It has more specific objectives. The officials not all, there are exceptions, by and large have been trained to conduct programmes for reporting. Of course, halls, public address system, food and refreshment have been provided just like for a wedding ceremony. For any training exercise, atmosphere is more important. The hall, public address system, the training material should create a sense to the participants that they have come for a serious purpose. First, training atmosphere could be created in the training place. It needs no money. It requires seriousness on the part of the organiser. The organiser's presence is also essential. The faculty felt that in some places organisers have taken keen interest in organising the programme. Organiser and his team were very much with the trainees. In most of the places organisers were not in the premises of the training centre and some subordinates have attended the work without knowing the importance and implications of the programme. This part needs a serious review.

Conclusion

The representatives of the people to the local bodies have now realised that they have more responsibilities than the previous period after attending this programme. The concept of power and authority has distorted the vision in the beginning. While explaining their responsibilities to create responsible citizens, they realised their tasks and works. It is an exercise to change the mind set of the women folk who have reached the portals of power. But this is only a beginning. This exercise has to continue. In the initial stage, for all training programme, institutions with faculty have been involved. But in the years to come the elected leaders who undergo training at present should be the master trainers. They are the pioneers in breaking new path for development. They are the agents of social transformation. This has to go a long way to achieve the objective of empowering the women for gender equity.

Coverage

Districts covered	16
Leaders trained	2150
Total No. of Municipalities	47
Total No. of Town Panchayats	267
Representatives from Municipalities	525
Representatives from Town Panchayats	1625
Total	2150

6

DEVELOPMENT FUNCTIONARIES PERCEPTION ON NEW PANCHAYATI RAJ SYSTEM

New Panchayati Raj System has been introduced with the specific objectives of economic development and social justice in rural area of our country. To fulfil the above mentioned objectives under the new Panchayati Raj, necessary powers and authorities are devolved to the various tiers of New Panchayati Raj system. Moreover the PRI administration is reorganised and reoriented for an effective and purposeful implementation of various schemes and programmes prepared by the people's representatives. The administrative power so far accumulated with the development functionaries are now decentralised and devolved to PRIs. In this context, there is a necessity of mind shift from the age old bureaucratic red tapism to new, transparent, positive and facilitating administration. Hence a study is carried out to understand the perception of development functionaries on New Panchayati Raj System.

Study Unit

Dindigul district is taken as the unit for this study. The sample respondents are from the district level to village Panchayat level Panchayati Raj functionaries.

Tool

An interview schedule is prepared and administered while interviewing the respondents selected randomly. Various aspects of new Panchayati Raj System like its aims and objectives, salient features of new system, major differences between the new and the old system, the decentralisation of power and authority, the relationship between official and non-official, fund allocation and utilisation, people's participation, political interference, empowerment of women and SC/ST under the new provision of reservation, power devolution in 29 subjects etc., are referred to in the interview schedule and the perception of respondents are recorded.

The following are the major findings revealed in the study:

1. It is reported that the major objectives of the new PR system are (i) power to the people, (ii) development by the people.
2. More power and responsibility is given to the people's representatives in the new system.
3. The role of development functionaries is minimised. The handling of money is now vested with the people's representatives.
4. Due to decentralisation, planning and execution of various schemes and programmes are quickly completed.
5. Development functionaries have undergone training in new PR system in which the aspects like administration, rules and regulations were oriented explained to them.
6. Devolution of power is exercised in various aspects like taxation, village plan preparation, selection of development schemes beneficiaries, handling of fund allocated to PRIs. Previously

the administrative sanctions have to be obtained from Panchayat union and district level officials. Now village Panchayats can pass resolution and take decision. Administrative sanction is not needed but only technical sanction is needed. This provide more opportunities to PRIs to decide the development programmes of their choice. The fund is deposited in the name of concerned PR institution.

7. The role and responsibility under each tier is properly explained to both officials and non-officials. Hence in general relationship between them is cordial. When rules and regulations are not adhered to by the non-officials in their respective day-to-day function, they are brought to their notice which may result in conflict. And in sometimes, the people's representatives wished to take development programmes very quickly and so they exerted pressure on the officials for immediate estimation, inspection or certification. Due to this there is a possibility of misunderstanding. Corruption prevails in any dealings. There will be misunderstanding between officials and non-officials over this issue.

8. The respondents generally have faith on the capability of non-officials in village planning. Moreover the other members have also participated and deliberated over the various schemes and programmes. It is possible for proper and meaningful planning exercise at each tier in the new system. A few respondents informed that most of the representatives are new comers, illiterates and semiliterates who are unable to understand and follow various guidelines in planning from below. Moreover, there is lack of technical knowledge and skill among the non-officials. Some respondents felt that if the village

panchayat members and president have preferences on caste, political party, religion, it will result in favouritism in planning and allocation of various schemes. Sometimes the entire hamlet is neglected by this negative approach.

9. The post of rural walfare officers are removed in the new system. They were the functionaries regularly visiting villages, collecting informations and acted as a link between village and government. Now there is no government servant for villagers except Panchayat clerk who is not a permanent full time worker.
10. The respondents opined that the existing arrangement of fund allocation is sufficient if the village plan is properly drafted every year.
11. The respondents felt that the funds are properly utilised, as the cheque operation is in joint account. There is a check at the village level. Moreover the accounts are verified and checked at the union level at every month.
12. It is referred that people's participation is less due to their indifferent experiences in PRIs i.e. the representatives are selfish, caste oriented or party oriented. People's welfare is set aside by the leaders. Even though there is a provision for people's participation in governance at local level "Gram Sabha" is never convened.
13. Common problems like street lights, drinking water, road, sanitation are somehow or otherwise dealt with under the village Panchayat level. People's perception is that PRI is there to provide facilities only and nothing more.
14. There are tender system in contract work and most of the contractors are belonging to various political parties. Hence there is political interference in PRIs. Moreover the election under

new system for Second and Third tier is on party basis.

15. Reservation to SC/ST women is very useful for their involvement. But women are not functioning independently. Those women who have family support, educated and already oriented in politics are independently functioning. Most of the women representatives are the family members of local party leaders. They do not have adequate knowledge and training in PR administration.
16. 29 subjects are still under discussion. No final devolution is announced by the state government.
17. Full time Panchayat secretary has to be appointed in each village Panchayat.

7

PARTICIPATION OF PEOPLE IN PROGRAMME AND TRAINING

INTRODUCTION

It is necessary that every issue affecting the human life could be seen in a wider context and analysed in the backdrop of the structural arrangements which we have established, nurtured and developed over a period of time. The escalating and insurmountable problems in the society indicate the weaknesses in the system and the managers who operate the system. To overcome the weaknesses in the system and the managers and to solve the problems, a new type of arrangement is being sought in the recent years, after seeing the overwhelming enthusiasm of the people in capturing the authoritative bodies. The competition for organisational power is an indicator of the people's desire to take up responsibility to manage their affairs and development on their own. The mechanism which has been created in the government to deliver goods to the people has demonstrated its inability, incapacity and insensitivity to the escalating human problems in the form of needs and expectations. All these changes in the world have compelled the countries to change over from the state oriented initiatives to people oriented development activities with involvement of people. Society moves from big government approach to small government approach and from sovereignty of state to empowerment of people. The ruling elites have to consider the global changes to activate the initiatives. This new situation warrants a fresh approach for the people to involve themselves in the development process.

PARTICIPATION OF PEOPLE IN THE PROGRAMME

From Community Development to Integrated Rural Development Programme, the government have adopted various nuances to involve people in the development process. Yet the initiatives have not really yielded results as both the ruling elites and the people (beneficiaries) have acted in a different mind set. The mind set that government is to give and people are to receive has pushed those two entities in different directions without taking them closer to work together to bring development. As a result the government has assumed several responsibilities and leaving the people with less amount of responsibility. This trend continued for about four decades which created a dependency syndrome on the part of the people. While analysing the programmes of the government especially with regard to the involvement of the people in the programmes and schemes for development, it is to be noted that there is no integrated document to give details regarding the schemes and programmes of many departments of the state and federal governments. Moreover the implementing agencies did not have elected local body institutions. As a result programmes are programmes of the officials for the benefit of the people which distanced the people from involving themselves in any stage of the development process from evolving schemes to evaluation of the same. The government thought about the estrangement of the people from the development process and tried to involve the people through an organised mechanism. Government has also created non-governmental societies like DRDA (District Rural Development Agencies) to involve people yet it became a government department in the course of its functioning. Even today many do not know that it is a registered society. Likewise the literacy mission 'Arivoli Iyakkam' is a movement for literacy which has also been created as an independent organisation to involve as much as people possible in the work to achieve the target. But it has been transformed into a government programme. Till date nobody knows why it has been called a movement? The above cited cases are mere examples. A large number of cases should be cited in this regard.

While implementing series of programmes, opportunities have been provided to the appropriate authorities to involve the people to identify the beneficiaries for schemes. Unfortunately while going through the practice at the level of government office in identifying the beneficiary, one would easily make a comment that most of the corrupt practices have been developed only in the process of identifying the beneficiary. Unless the norms and conditions are popularised the beneficiaries may not know the details and the individuals who have got vested interest will continue to thrive in the process and by which corrupt bullies will emerge and control the delivery system. Hence as of today the involvement of the people in the programme is almost a farce and it has to be seen in a new context.

PROGRAMMES IN THE NEW CONTEXT

Decentralization of power, planning from the below and participation of people in the planning process amply demonstrate that more number of programmes have to be evolved locally with the involvement of the people. The practice of continuing the same old pattern of proliferating centrally sponsored schemes and state evolved schemes for rural development has to be abrogated. More programmes and schemes have to be evolved locally within the broad framework of the federal and state planning commissions. While giving power to evolve more number of programmes and schemes, equally power should be given to local bodies to mobilise resource from the local areas by which both governments can withdraw from the responsibility of meeting local specific needs. The tendency of giving money from the above for all the programmes and schemes would continue the practice of perpetuating the dependency syndrome on the part of the people. Moreover the mind set of the present elected local body leaders that the local body leaders have to act as an agent to receive the doles from the government and distribute them to the people as MLAs or MPs, has to be changed. Unless the mind set of the leaders is changed, the very purpose of constitutionalising the local body will be defeated. Further the local level planning should be based on the availability of local resources, local skills and environmental conditions. The local body institutions should take up the responsibility of building up the resourcefulness of the people by improving the knowledge and skill of the people.

OBSTACLES TO PARTICIPATION

Obstacles are many in involving the people in all the stages of development programmes and schemes such as planning, implementation and evaluation. In the given situation any organisation which can enlist the participation of people do not have the belief that the people can do and achieve things. As far as the government machinery is concerned the people are to receive and government has to provide. Moreover the increasing number of government offices with the given mind set that officials can do and people cannot do, have done harm to the very process of initiative to involve the people. Obsolete and outmoded structures have to be weeded out from the rubric of administration. The presence of unwanted and obsolete structures will always be an impediment to the progress of the society. The New Panchayati Raj system is not merely an administrative reform measure. It is a mass movement by itself. The involvement is not a piece meal activity. It should be total with the hope that they are going to succeed. They should have the feeling that they are the initiators. Even at the office level information is not freely shared among the elected leaders and between the leaders and the officials about the facilities, schemes and programmes available at their hands for the benefit of the people. Since there is no identifiable source to get to know the details of all the programmes and schemes, people do not evince any interest in the programmes which ultimately relegate the people and their leaders to the background. To remove all obstacles a package of programmes has to be introduced. Of them training is the most important one.

TRAINING NEED

To get the best from the leaders, training is an imperative need. Training is not a one time programme. It is a continuous programme. Training need varies from cadre to cadre. Village Panchayat needs training for its leaders and members. Likewise the members and leaders of the other tiers of the rural local bodies and urban bodies need such training. Each tier has to perform certain duties and responsibilities as per the provisions of the acts of the government. The varying degrees of duties and responsibilities of the members and leaders require specific and appropriate training to perform their duties effectively.

Training should be given not only for the elected leaders but also to the officials who work in the local bodies. The officials at different levels from secretariat to Panchayati Union need training or orientation. Course packages have to be evolved to train the local body leaders and other functionaries. First a general awareness could be created among the public about the New Panchayati Raj System. It should be explained not in abstracts term but in context relating to the existing socio-economic and political conditions of the country and the world. A general course module has to be prepared. Based on the assigned duties to the local body leaders, course module has to be evolved and imparted to all. The training programmes should cover, skill, knowledge behaviour and functions or tasks.

The local body institution has to perform the following functions:

1. Provide facilities to the people;
2. Use the facilities for economic growth;
3. Train the people in the art of democratic governance;
4. Train the people in citizenry;
5. Train the people to manage their affairs on their own;
6. Train the people in community action;
7. Train the people in local resource mobilization;
8. Reduce the workload of the higher governments;
9. Bring transparency in the activities of the local bodies;

10. Train the people in micro level planning; and
11. Bring closeness between the people and the government.

To perform the above mentioned tasks training should be offered to village panchayati presidents and vice-presidents, panchayati union chair-persons and vice-chairpersons, district Panchayati chair-persons and vice-chairpersons, chair-persons and vice-chairpersons of town panchayats, chair-persons and vice-chairpersons of municipalities and mayors and deputy mayors of corporations. Likewise the officials working in all the offices have to be trained. Those who involve in decision making process from federal government to state government, will be given orientation. Depending upon the need and assigned duties and responsibilities orientations have to be given. On four fronts they are to be changed namely, attitude, behaviour, skill and performance.

For each segment module has to be developed for training. A few examples will be of much use for evolving modules for other section. First to offer training to all the segments master trainers have to be trained. The master trainers programme should have the following objects:

Module I

Master Trainers Programme

1. To enable the participants to know the emerging trends in Panchayati Raj System in the country and the role which these bodies are expected to play in the overall implementation of various development programmes as a result of the 73rd Constitutional Amendment;
2. To facilitate the participants in gaining an

understanding of the management of Panchayati Raj Institutions at different levels of administration i.e., Village Panchayat, Panchayati Union and District Panchayat;

3. To develop knowledge and competence in the use of various training methods and aids; and
4. To prepare them for imparting further training to the different categories of elected representatives.

Course Content

1. Brief History of Panchayati Raj in India.
2. Salient features of the 73rd Amendment Act.
3. Salient features of the Tamil Nadu Local Body Act 1994.
4. People's participation
   a) The Centralisation and decentralisation of power.
   b) Participatory approach to development.
   c) Role of MPs, MLAs and local body leaders in development.
   d) Approaches to increasing people's participation.
5. Organisation set-up for planning, implementation and evaluation.
6. Mobilisation of people for participation in planning, implementation and monitoring.
7. Analysis of the responsibility of the elected leaders and the other functionaries on the subjects mentioned in eleventh schedule and twelfth schedule.
8. Interlinkages between local bodies and other developmental organisations.
9. Analysis of resource mobilisation.
10. Development of weaker sections.
11. Analysing micro level planning.
12. Linkage between National, State, District, Union

and Village level plans.

13. Planning process.
14. Common property resource management.
15. Rural development programmes.
16. Rural urban nexus.

Training technique:

Methodology: The training methods will include

* lecture-cum-discussion
* case studies
* exercises
* field trips

Audio visual methods will be employed to conduct the training programme.

Module II

President and Vice-President of District Panchayat

1. *Course Contents*

1.1 General Orientation

a) Plan process in the country

b) Democratic decentralization

c) Rural development programmes

1.2 Subject Orientation

a) Panchayati Raj: Concept and Status

b) Salient features of Panchayati Raj structure in the concerned State-Gram Sabha, Village Panchayat, Panchayat Union and District Panchayat.

c) Functions of District Panchayat with particular reference to

i) Formation of Standing Committee;

ii) Planning and Implementation of District Level Plans;

iii) Management of rural development

schemes; and

iv) Moitoring and evaluation.

d) Resource of District Panchayat

e) Staff of District Panchayat

f) Supervision and control over Panchayat Unions and Village Panchayats

1.3 Role Orientation/Behavioural Aspects

a) Role and responsibilities and elected representatives at District level.

b) Role and responsibilities of officials at the district level.

c) Relationship between officials at the district level.

1.4 Activity Orientation

All 29 subjects in the eleventh schedule.

1.5 Management Orientation

a) Administrative coordination with different panchayat samities.

b) . Role of district panchayat in planning and development

c) Role of district level officials

d) Decentralised planning

i) Preparation of plans

ii) Identification of resources

iii) Data base

e) Implementation of special programmes

f) Budget of district panchayat

g) Powers and functions of district panchayat

h) Resource mobilisation

i) Conduct of business

i) Meeting of district panchayat

ii) Agenda

iii) Vote of no confidence

iv) Disqualification of members

v) Quorum

vi) Minutes of meeting

j) Training of officials/non-officials

k) Personnel administration

l) Maintenance of properties of district panchayats

m) Management of primary schools

1.6 Field Orientation

Visits to some successful institutions, demonstration farms, programme. The objective is essentially educative and to expose the trainees to successful projects. Visits may be arranged to model Panchayats and to knowledgeable individuals, social workers in nearby areas or to a cooperative bank.

A. Illustrative list of Institutions/Organisations/ Projects

1. A successful panchayat
2. A successful cooperative society
3. Farmer's mandal, mahila mandal
4. A cooperative bank
5. Agriculture research farm/Seed multiplication farm
6. Dairy farm, cattle and poultry farms
7. Afforestation programme
8. Cottage and village industries centres etc.

B. Projects

1. An irrigation or Hydel project
2. A key industry
3. A model housing colony

C. Individuals

1. A successful farmer
2. A successful cattle breeder and poultry breeder

Module III

Chairman and Vice-Chairman of Panchayati Union

1. *Course Contents*

1.1 General Orientation
- a) Plan process in the country
- b) Rural development programmes
- c) Democratic decentralization

1.2 Subject Orientation
- a) Panchayati Raj: Concept and status
- b) Salient features of Panchayati Raj structure in the concerned State-Gram Sabha, Village Panchayat, Panchayat Union and District Panchayat.
- c) Functions of District Panchayat with particular reference to
  - i) Planning and Implementation of Block level Plans
  - ii) Management of rural development schemes and
  - iii) Monitoring and evaluation
- d) Resource of Panchayat Union
- e) Role and responsibilities of staff of Panchayati union
- f) Supervision and control over Village Panchayats

1.3 Role Orientation/Behavioural Aspects
- a) Role and responsibilities and elected representatives
- b) Role and responsibilities of officials
- c) Relationship between officials and elected representatives
- d) Community contacts

1.4 Activity Orientation

All 29 subjects in the eleventh schedule.

1.5 Management Orientation

a) Team work
b) Administrative coordination with District Panchayat and different Panchayats
c) Emerging role of Panchayat Union in planning and development
d) Role of block level officials
e) Maintenance of records
f) Preparation of block level plans
g) Coordination of village-level plans
h) Implementation of special programmes
i) Panchayat Union budget
j) Audit and accounts
k) Resource mobilization
l) Conduct of business
   i) Meeting of Panchayat Union
   ii) Preparation of Agenda
   iii) Vote of no confidence
   iv) Disqualification of members
   v) Quorum
   vi) Minutes of meeting
m) State Government agencies operating at State/District/Block level
n) Agencies operating within District such as banks/cooperatives and voluntary organisations
o) Preservation of common property
p) Management of public utility services

1.6 Field Orientation

Visits to some successful institutions, demonstration farms, programme. The objective is essentially educative and to expose the trainees to successful projects. Visits may be arranged to model Panchayats and to knowledgeable individuals, social workers in nearby areas or to a cooperative bank.

A. Illustrative list of Institutions/Organisations/ Projects
   1. A successful panchayat
   2. A successful cooperative society
   3. Farmer's mandal, mahila mandal
   4. A cooperative bank
   5. Agriculture research farm/Seed multiplication farm
   6. Dairy farm, cattle and poultry farms
   7. Afforestation programme
   8. Cottage and village industries centres etc.

B. Projects
   1. An irrigation or Hydel project
   2. A key industry
   3. A model housing colony etc.

C. Individuals
   1. A successful farmer
   2. A successful cattle breeder and poultry breeder
   3. An Anganwadi worker

Module IV

President and Vice-President of Village Panchayat

1. *Course Contents*

1.1 General Orientation
   a) Plan process in the country
   b) Rural development programmes
   c) Democratic decentralisation

1.2 Subject Orientation
   a) Panchayati Raj: Concept and status
   b) Salient features of Panchayati Raj structure in the concerned State-Gram Sabha, Village Panchayat, Panchayat Union and District Panchayat.
   c) Functions of District Panchayat with

particular reference to

i) Planning and Implementation of Block level Plans

ii) Management of rural development schemes and

iii) Moitoring and evaluation

d) Resource of Panchayat Union

e) Role and responsibilities of staff of Panchayati union

f) Supervision and control over Village Panchayats

1.3 Role Orientation/Behavioural Aspects

a) Role and responsibilities and elected representatives at village level

b) Role and responsibilities of officials level

c) Relationship between officials and elected representatives

d) Collective leadership and people's participation

e) Experience sharing

f) Team work

1.4 Activity Orientation

All 29 subjects in the eleventh schedule.

1.5 Management Orientation

a) Administrative management of programmes in Panchayat Union

b) Emerging role of Panchayats in planning and development

c) Maintenance of records

d) Preparation of village plans

e) Implementation of special programmes

f) Panchayat fund and budget

g) Maintenance of accounts

h) Audit and Accounts

i) Resource mobilization

j) Conduct of business

i) Meeting of Gram Sabha
ii) Meeting of Panchayats
iii) Preparation of Agenda
iv) Disqualification of members
v) Vote of no confidence
vi) Quorum
vii) Minutes of meeting

k) State Government agencies operating at State/District/Block level
l) Agencies operating within District such as banks/cooperatives and voluntary organisations
m) Protection of community lands
n) Management of primary schools

1.6 Field Orientation

Visits to some successful institutions, demonstration farms, programmes to educate and to expose the trainees to successful projects will be required. This may include successful Panchayats and to knowledgeable individuals, social workers or a cooperative bank in nearby areas.

A. Illustrative list of Institutions/Organisations/Projects

1. A successful panchayat
2. A successful cooperative society
3. Farmer's mandal, mahila mandal
4. A cooperative bank
5. Agriculture research farm/Seed multiplication farm
6. Dairy farm, cattle and poultry farms
7. Afforestation programme
8. Cottage and village industries centres etc.

B. Projects

1. An irrigation or Hydel project
2. A key industry

3. A model housing colony etc.

C. Individuals
1. A successful farmer
2. A successful cattle breeder and poultry breeder
3. An Anganwadi worker

Methodology
1. Lecture method
2. Discussion
3. Field Visits/Demonstration

Module V

Panchayat Union Level Functionaries

1. *Course contents*

1.1 General Orientation
a) Socio economic conditions of rural India
b) Functioning of bureaucracy
c) Democratic decentralization
d) Rural development programmes
e) Plan process in the country

1.2 Subject Orientation
a) Panchayati Raj: Concept and status
b) Salient features of Panchayati Raj structure in the concerned State-Gram Sabha, Village Panchayat, Panchayat Union and District Panchayat.
c) Functions of District Panchayat with particular reference to
   i) Planning and Implementation of Block level Plans;
   ii) Management of rural development schemes; and
   iii) Monitoring and evaluation
d) Resource of Panchayat Union
e) Role and responsibilities of staff of Panchayati

union

f) Supervision and control over Village Panchayats

1.3 Role Orientation/Behavioural Aspects

a) Rules with reference to service matters
b) Role and responsibilities of officials at village level
c) Interface between officials and non-officials
d) Code of conduct for officials and non-officials.
e) Public relations.

1.4 Activity Orientation

All 29 subjects in the eleventh schedule.

1.5 Management Orientation

a) Team work - horizontal and vertical coordination; administration; integration; linkages.
b) Office management — maintenance of records and files.
c) Preparation of village plan/block plan.
d) Implementation of special programme.
e) Budget of Panchayat union.
f) Audit and accounts.
g) Resource mobilization.
h) Innovative experiments in administration and development.
i) Conduct of meetings.
j) Inter- and intra-departmental agencies and linkages.
k) Role of non-governmental organisations.
l) Management of public utility services.
m) Preservation of common property resources.
n) Social audit and public accountability.
o) Environmental education.

1.6 Field Orientation

Visits to some successful institutions, demonstration farms, programmes. The objective is essentially to educate and expose the trainees to successful projects/programmes for schemes. Visits may be arranged to some model unions and to knowledgeable individuals, social workers of the area. In addition to this film shows, audio-visual methods would be used to provide an understanding with regard to the procedures and processes relating to various activities of the unions.

A. Illustrative list of Institutions/Organisations/ Projects
   1. A successful panchayat
   2. A successful cooperative society
   3. Farmer's mandal, mahila mandal
   4. A cooperative bank
   5. Agriculture research farm/Seed multiplication farm
   6. Dairy farm, cattle and poultry farms
   7. Afforestation programme
   8. Cottage and village industries centres etc.

B. Projects
   1. An irrigation or Hydel project
   2. A key industry
   3. A model housing colony
   4. A successful poverty alleviation programme

C. Individuals
   1. A successful farmer/small entrepreneur/ beneficiary.

Module VI

Training Module for Training of Trainers of Panchayati Raj Functionaries

Objectives

1. To enable the participants to know the emerging trends in the Panchayati Raj System in the

country and the role which these bodies are expected to play in the overall implementation of various development programmes as a result of 73rd Constitutional Amendment.

2. To facilitate the participants in gaining an understanding of the management of Panchayati Raj Institutions at different levels of administration i.e., Village Panchayat, Panchayat Union and District Panchayat.
3. To develop knowledge and competence in the use of various training methods and aids.
4. To prepare them for imparting further training to the different categories of elected representatives.

Course Content

1.1 Brief resume of Panchayati Raj in India.

1.2 Salient features of 73rd Constitution.

1.3 Salient features of Panchayati Raj Act of the concerned Act (Emphasis will be mainly on highlighting salient features of differences between 73rd Constitution Amendment and the Panchayati Raj Act under reference).

1.4 People's participation:
- a) Concept of democratic decentralisation
- b) Participatory approaches to development
- c) Role of MPs/MLAs
- d) Approaches for optimising people's participation

1.5 Organisational set-up of District Planning and Development Administration with particular reference to 74th Constitution Amendment and the District Planning Committee. General functioning of various development departments and line of control of district and sub-district levels, their relations with Panchayati Raj bodies.

1.6 Approaches to planning in respect of developmental responsibilities given to Panchayati Raj bodies vis-a-vis mobilisation of people's participation in planning, implementation and monitoring.

1.7 Analysis of functions entrusted to Panchayati Raj bodies with particular reference to 11th schedule of the constitution and Panchayati Raj act of the concerned state.

1.8 Inter-linkages between Panchayati Raj bodies and other organisations such as Banks, Cooperatives and Voluntary organizations.

1.9 Resource Analysis: Potential and current availability of resources all the disposal of Panchayati Raj bodies.

2.0 Comprehensive review of government rules to safeguard the interest of specific sections of population i.e., SC, ST women.

2.1 Brief review of micro level planning experiences (district/block/village).

2.2 Linkages between National/State/District/ Block/Village plans. District planning committee — Scope and operational dimensions.

2.3 Planning methodologies including situation analysis, use of information base, graphics, study of spatial linkages, methodologies to formulate objectives (short and long term), formulation of plans covering components like: (i) Development goals, (ii) Resource support, (iii) Plan programming and integration of programmes, (iv) Time frame, (v) People's involvement at all stages of development including gender issues.

2.4 Management of property, assets and funds. Audit and accounting plan implementation.

identification of constraints.

2.5 Rural development programmes, strategies and approaches.

2.6 Poverty alleviation and employment generation in rural areas — critical issues and problems.

2.7 Rural-Urban linkages.

2.8 Monitoring and evaluation.

2.9 Training of officials and non-officials at block and village levels.

3.0 Training Modules for officials and non-officials at different levels of Panchayati Raj administration.

3.1 Assessment of training needs of first time leadership among SC and ST population and women.

3.2 Training techniques.

3.3 Evaluation of training programme.

3.4 Women and SC, ST in Panchayati Raj.

3.5 Role of Panchayati Raj institutions in literacy.

Participants

The course is intended for Heads and Senior Faculty of the apex level institutions and other resource persons used by them in their training programmes (as designated by the State Government, be it SIRD or GRI or some other institution), teachers drawn from universities, colleges and institutions etc., who are potential trainers and even functional heads associated with training programmes under the reference.

All Training programmes will have the following common features:

Number of Trainees : 35
Duration : 5 days

Institutions	:	NIRD/SIRD/GRI, Gandhigram/Tamil Nadu Institute of Urban Studies/ Extension Training Centres/Selected NGOs
	:	Fully residential
Daily schedule	:	
Lecture Sessions	:	9.30 - 12.30
Lunch	:	12.30 - 14.30
Discussion session	:	14.30 - 16.00
Practical work/ Field visits	:	16.00 - 19.00
Dinner	:	19.00 - 20.00
Video and Social & Cultural Programmes	:	20.00 - 22.00

All the above modules are drawn from NIRD exercises. Some modifications have been made to suit the local conditions. Based on these modules training has been started by Gandhigram Rural Institute to train the Village Panchayati Presidents with the financial support of CAPART.

8

STATE-LOCAL GOVERNMENTS RELATIONS IN TAMIL NADU

Introduction

In the fifty years of democratic governance, a variety of models of development have been experimented to achieve equity, growth and development in the Indian society by the state authorities. Yet the promises of the founding fathers and goals of our nation have not been realised and the governing machineries have undergone stress and strain. The appalling conditions have propelled the leaders of the government to think of an alternative arrangement to manage the existing socio-economic crises and administer development. The fifth decade of Indian Federalism has opened up a new chapter in the annals of institutions of governance in India. Creation of an institution arrangement at the grass-root level through the Constitution of India for governance with earmarked powers, responsibilities and subjects signifies a marked departure from the conventional thinking of federalism. Conventional federalism emphatically establishes relationship between the federal and provincial governments. In India, even before the advent of federalist thinking among the founding fathers at the dawn of Independence the exponents of Federalism Harold Laski and K.C. Wheare had started doubting the efficiency and efficacy of the Federal institutional arrangement in delivering their goods. For about four decades the federal polity had undergone a metamorphosis and finally resulted in creating a new institutional arrangement at the bottom of the society for governance. It is almost a paradigmatic shift from the centre-state relations to state-local government relations which determines the development process of the society. While looking at the functioning of the local body institutions one would find many contradictions as mode of production and economic activities have been centralised. This contradictory position repeatedly gives room for declaration of new proposition that a thorough change in Constitution alone can make the society to prosper and maintain equity. Any way the focus has come to the linkages between the state and local bodies.

The Issue

In the fifty years of political socialization process, the roots of democratic politics have gone deep into the Indian soil and thereby every issue is visualised rationally both economically and socially by the people of this country. Emergence of coalition politics at the national level and emergence of more number of caste groups in the regional politics have altered the paradigm of Indian Political System. The equation between micro politics and macro politics had been visualised from the perspective of the dominant paradigm of influencing the politics of the rural areas by the policy options of the federal and state governments for about four decades. But now the national polity is being influenced by the regional polities and regional polities are influenced by the sub-regional polities. Thus power equations have been changed topsy turvily. At this juncture power equations between the centre and states have not drawn the attention of the scholars and the politicians as the federal government is being managed by the regional parties and the relationship between the state and local bodies has gained momentum and the sub-regional political parties and national political parties demand more powers to the local bodies. This new phenomenon draws the attention of the hard core academics to locate the anchorage of power. The problem before us at present in power sharing is the obstacle in the passage of powers from the states to the local bodies. This study underlines the problematic areas in the decentralization process.

Theoretical Framework

It is obvious that the power relations are dominantly influenced by mode of production and environmental conditions of international order and power equations are always based on the control of resources. Concentration of power coterminous with concentration of resources. The Indian state was born in an alarmist situation which resulted in building a strong state through the Constitution. The Indian National Congress as a political party came to power and halted in power for an unshakable term for about two decades and had not given rise to any rift between the centre and the state in an alarmist proportion. The centre-state relations gained momentum after the regional political parties assumed power in some of the regions. The Indian National Congress also heard the voice of dissent vociferously from its own regional leaders against the party high command. In 1960's and 1970's the centre had started taking away the powers of the states despite the powerful demand of the provincial governments. During the period of centralization of powers, resource concentration has been anchored at the centre. To get adequate resources for the development activities of the provinces, the parties in the state have to please the centre instead of displeasing the centre by raising the demand for powers. Even the resources have been granted with the spelt out schemes and programmes. Thus state governments were made as agencies to implement central government programmes and schemes.

In the slow process of centralization of power by the federal government, the state government has followed the pattern of the centre and started taking away the power of the local bodies. Centralization of power from local bodies to state and from state to the centre has helped the bureaucracy to amass wealth and flout rules and regulations as the governing process distanced the people from understanding the governance. Thus the socio-economic problems of the people have not been properly attended to by the government and as a result the anti-establishment sentiments have grown among the people. The continuous political mobilization of the people by the political parties have revised hopes and aspirations of the people. When the big governments have not met the aspirations and hopes of the people, anti-establishment sentiments have increased. As a result of which more number of sub-regional parties based on caste, class and tribe have emerged. Local issues have been used. Concentration of financial powers at the centre through Planning Commission, allocation of resources to provinces through schemes made the state governments as implementing agencies. The state planning commissions or boards are to make proposals to get money from the Planning Commission within the framework of schemes and programmes earmarked by the central government. By making the state government to perform the agency functions, the central government has a supervisory role to stipulate conditions and hold or withhold the allocation of money for state governments based on performance appraisal.

Concentration of powers at the centre helped the few sections to make use of the policy options of the governments and the absence of popular institutional mechanisms. As a result major sections of the people were driven away from the market as active participants both as producer and consumer. The centralization process has driven the dominant national forces away from power and the regional forces have joined together to take up the mantle of the national forces. In the same pattern the regional forces are put into trouble by the sub-regional forces. Totally anti-establishment sentiment has formed among the collectivities.

To change the situation an alternative was devised and it is called "decentralization of power". To free the people from the control of the state and to enable the people to participate in the market as producer and consumer a new arrangement of governance has been introduced in the New Panchayati Raj System. The new arrangement has been evolved only when constraints on state, market and resources have been exhibited. By the new dispensation one would witness the draining of the rest of powers from the provincial government and make it only a gatevalve for the flow of powers and resources. The present hurdles and deterrents are due to the fear that state government will be marginalized. Against this background the whole issue of the state and local body relationship has to be visualised.

Examination of the Cases

First the whole of decentralization of powers has been carried out through the centralization process. Devolution of powers has taken shape neither based on the demand of the people nor on the will of the provincial government leader excepting West Bengal. Devolution of powers took place with much resistance after the introduction of the 73rd constitutional Amendment. At present when mode of production is highly concentrated, devolution of powers meant sharing of resources. Hence MPs have taken part in resource sharing through their Area development programme. MLAs have also joined them to take another share from the same resource pool for the same work. Rest of the resources have been devolved to the local bodies. Since the federal government treated the provincial government as implementing agencies, the same has been the perception of the provincial government over the local bodies. Since the largeness of the government is visible, people have relegated their responsibilities. The slow but steady process of usurping the powers and responsibilities of the people by the government helped the governments especially the federal government to perform the local body functions and for which they sought loans from world level funding agencies.

Further competition for welfare programmes between the provincial governments and Federal Government further intensified the alienation of power centre from the people and all the welfare programmes have been operated only by the officials. The poor attention paid by the officials in collecting local taxes, leaving the commons without any proper attention have completely eroded the bases of local body institutions.

At this juncture steps had been taken to revitalise the grass-root level institutions for governance. 73rd constitutional amendment has provided a framework for devolution of powers. This process again is a game plan between the centre and the states. 73rd amendment stipulates certain conditions for the creation of local body institutions. The state governments which have got will power have implemented the 73rd constitutional amendment more than the expectations of the proponents of 73rd constitutional amendment. Particularly in Tamil Nadu, the will of the leaders were against the devolution of powers to local bodies and hence a bill passed in the year 1994 negated the spirit of the constitutional amendment. Tamil Nadu Government had determined not to conduct the elections and as a result the Federal Government threatened the state government that it would cut the grant for rural development activities. Despite this threat, election was not conducted. The local body election was conducted in time with the promises given by the present ruling party the DMK. Mere conduct of election does not help the local bodies.

Establishment of local body institutions means creation of a self governing institution with a package of programmes. But in Tamil Nadu it is considered as a scheme without devolving overt powers for decision making. When powers are devolved they should be in line with the spirit of the 73rd Constitutional Amendment Act. A committee has been constituted to work out the modalities to devolve powers to the three tiers of the local bodies under the chairmanship of L.C. Jain. The committee has submitted its interim as well as final report but yet actions are to be taken in tune with the recommendations of the committee. Micro level planning is the vital aspect of the New Panchayati

Raj System. The Government order says that the District Collector is the chair-person of the District Planning Committee. DRDA is a society registered with the registrar of societies office and it should become infructuous when District Panchayat takes up the responsibilities.

But the whole developmental activities are carried out only through DRDA and all the powers related to the functioning of DRDA are vested with the District Collector. District Collector is the representative of the State Government as the Governor to the State from the federal government. For financial resources they have to rely on the state government as the state government rely on the federal government. Only in the recent past the state government has established its higher claim in the tax share with the federal government. The state government has fixed 8% of share in the tax collection for local bodies. Establishing administrative control over the Panchayats has increased tremendously as money flow increased. The attitude of the state government towards the Panchayati bodies is the reflection of the attitude of the central government towards the state government. As the federal government is represented by more number of regional political parties and national political parties which have faith in decentralization, the devolution of powers do not irritate both. The same would have been a different one if the central government is in the hands of a dominant national political party.

Inferences

Decentralization of powers or devolution of powers takes place in a centralized manner. Decentralization of powers is a major tensional area between the centre and the state. For state autonomy near about three decades the regional political parties fought and thereby the federal government has started taking away some of the powers of the state. In the same way the state governments have taken away the powers of the local bodies.

In the critical juncture of market expansion more number of human collectivities have to be brought under the fold of market which needs liberation of the people from the state, adjustment devices in the structure to enable the economic forces to penetrate into the society and to increase the capacity of the people to make use of the resources and institutions to achieve development and for which devolution of powers is more important. Devolution of powers, increasing the resourcefulness of the people, small government, good governance and corruption free government are the mandatory propositions of the funding agencies of the world. This decentralization is for centralization of economic powers through decentralised economic activities. The state government has been adopting the strategies to devolve powers as the federal government has been adopting for decentralization of power from the centre to the state.

Finance is the key factor which determines the relationship between the centre and the state. Likewise the state government makes the Panchayats as dependent on the state government for financial allocation. Yet another factor, namely political will rather than the constitutional provision plays a determinant role in devolving powers. As long as Jawaharlal Nehru was the Prime Minister, our federal government was functionally oriented towards community, welfare and development. The leaders will is more important for decentralization of power. Decentralization of power is perceived as devolution of powers from the state to the local bodies and not from the centre to the state. Decentralization of power really means flow of power from the centre to the state and state to local bodies. Unless the powers are devolved from the federal government to the provincial government, one would not expect any meaningful flow of powers and resources to local bodies from the state government.

Conclusion

Centre-state relations acquired prominence in the discussions of the academics for about three decades which has no attraction now even though powers are not transferred to the state and at present the forces have come to state-local body relationship. Devolution of powers is not an isolated event in the transformation process. It is a package of activities but the state governments, have been adopting the methodology of the federal government in devolving powers.

This decentralization process takes place at a juncture of extreme centralization of economic powers. More than the provisions political will determines the nature and speed of flow of powers. Understanding the context and concept, 'decentralization process' could be effected to achieve peace and development otherwise it would bring more conflict in the rural areas. More particularly it would help the concentration of economic power.

9

LINKAGES OF THE SERVICES OF THE REPRESENTATIVES OF THE PEOPLE

Introduction

Empowering people through the 73rd Amendment to the Constitution of India has entrusted more responsibilities on the people to take care of the local problems on their own with the resources available with and provided to them from the federal and state governments. After instituting a new arrangement of governance at the local level to involve more number of people to tackle their own problems, the concept of representation in Indian parliamentary democracy gets a new dimension. While allocating power and authority to leaders of local bodies through an amendment to the constitution of India, the representatives at the national parliament have posited a demand of share in resource allocation to meet the demands of the constituents. This demand was considered positively and granted one crore rupees to every M.P. for development activities in the respective constituencies of the representatives.

Following the decision of the federal government, the state legislatures embarked in enacting suitable legislation in accordance with the amendment to the Constitution of India. Members of state legislature have also started posing such demands and thereby some of the state governments have provided funds for them to take up development activities. These activities have to be carried out only through the district administration. By making this provision, the legislators have been provided with executive powers.

This programme meant was for MPs called "MPs Local Area Development Scheme". Under the scheme, each member of parliament will have the freedom to suggest to the District Collector works to be done not exceeding rupees one crore every year within his/her constituency. Members of Lok Sabha can undertake works in their respective constituencies and likewise the Rajya Sabha members can select a district in the state wherefrom he or she has been elected or nominated to Rajya Sabha. As per the specification of the scheme, fund has to be utilised by the district collector with the direction of the MPs. Moreover the MP's will have a chance to participate in the deliberations of the district and Block Panchayat systems. Hence a Member of Parliament can work effectively in unison with other representatives of the local areas to fulfil the needs of the people. The linkage are functional in nature.

The critical question is, whether the representatives of the people can work effectively with the people as they are in different bodies as representatives of political parties at different levels. Further if one assumes that they are working together to solve the problems of the people by sinking their differences, what are the operational areas where they can work together to solve the problems of the constituents? These are the questions addressed in this chapter. The above posited questions will be examined in this chapter and attempts are made here to evolve a framework to establish a dynamic operational linkage between the representatives of the people serving in national and regional bodies and the representatives of the local bodies within the constitutional framework.

A Framework for Representatives Actions

A geographical area has been represented by many representatives in different authoritative bodies. A district is represented by district Panchayat president, MPs, MLAs, district Panchayat council members, Panchayati union chair-persons, Panchayati union council members, Gram Panchayati presidents and Gram Panchayat ward members. All these representatives are working in the respective constituencies for the well-being of the constituents. But all the representatives have not been functioning in consonance with the role specified for them. The demarcation of role and function is based on the classification of the subjects to all the three centres of powers namely the federal government, provincial government and local government. Subjects are classified in three heads namely central list, state list and concurrent list. Now one more list is included. There are overlapping categories. Despite all those classification of subjects, roles and functions, the performance of the representatives has not solved the problems of the people. The critical examination of the performance of the governments both at the federal and provincial levels has led to the introduction of the new Panchayati Raj system. This New Panchayati Raj System will reduce the government structure above the local bodies and take up more responsibilities from the state and federal governments. The devolution of power along with increasing allocation of money to local bodies appears that the local body institutions and representatives gain momentum and popularity among the people.

People who have problems will approach the representatives. People won't classify their issues and approach the appropriate representatives based on the nature of issues. Whether the subject is central or state or local government, people use to represent to the representatives who are nearer to them irrespective of their positions. A large number of members of parliament has approached the federal government to earmark powers to recommend to the District Collector for small works to be done for their consituencies. Likewise the members of Legislative Assembly have also posited such demands. All these demands were raised in the context of devolution of powers and resources to the local body institutions. The question is whether the act of the federal government and the state governments in allowing the members of parliament and state legislatures to share power and resources with the representatives of the local body is correct as per the logic of the devolution of powers. Since powers have been given to MPs and MLAs to share the resources with local body members, how it should be done is the major issue to be discussed.

The representatives of the people have two major functions namely interest aggregation and interest articulations. From local body institutions to National Parliament, the representatives have to collect the demands and grievances of the people and they should be given proper policy shape before they will be presented in appropriate authoritative bodies for decision making and policy making. But now the parliamentary institutions and their members have been given executive powers. They are given money to perform certain functions other than the earmarked functions in authoritative bodies.

A representative (Members of Parliament) can chalk out a plan to utilise one crore rupees every year in administering development. Each representative should have a thorough understanding of the problems of his or her constituency. After his assessment, he has to identify the works to be carried out in the constituency as per the specifications given in the scheme order. He has to specify the problems for which he has to spend the earmarked money. Of the issues, problems relating to health draw the attention of all. Simultaneously the representatives have to get to know the details regarding the allocation of money for various works from the amount allotted to MLA under this new scheme. Likewise the representatives should be aware of various schemes implemented by the central and state governments apart from various agencies like NGO. The list of works indicated in the MP's Local Area Development Scheme is only a suggestive one. It can be expanded. Prior to utilization, proper diagnosis of the problems, issues and ills in the society is needed. Schemes and programmes flow to the district should be known to the member of parliament. Likewise programmes and schemes flow to the taluk or the constituency level should be known to the members of Legislative Assembly also.

In the years to come all villages will have a document portraying the problems issues and priorities of the people. How these problems are going to be solved through the schemes and programmes apart from the schemes and programmes to be evolved by the Panchayats in the process of planning at the grass-roots level?

Multiplicity of representatives in a given constituency with executive powers have caused imbalance in allocation of resources and works. To avoid such imbalance of allocation of resources and works, representatives have to make realistic assessment of needs. It could be done both by the concerned representative and the officials who involve in administering development. If the assessment is done by the concerned individual representative, it will be of much use for them to contribute for policy and decision making.

Panchayati Raj becomes a reality, all those service and productive activities could be carried out only through these bodies. In the district planning committee, all those schemes and works of representatives could be properly discussed and placed approximately in the plan document and those works and schemes could be executed systematically without any imbalance.

The representatives of the people have more responsibilities in the society and polity. They should not consider that allocating resources and approving the schemes are the functions of member of parliament. They should have adequate information on issues and problems of the people to be placed before the authoritative bodies for decision making. At the same time they have to educate the people by their visits and meetings with the people. A self explanatory diagram protrays the relationship.

District		District
	District Panchayat	
M.P.	Ward Member, Vice-President,	President
	Panchayat Union	
M.L.A.	Union Council, Vice-Chairman,	Chairman
	Gram Panchayat	
	Ward Members, Vice-President,	President
District		District

Conclusion

A large number of representatives of the people are working in three different systems namely National

Parliament, State Legislatures and Panchayati Bodies. In a district roughly two MPs (it varies from state to state) more than ten MLAs, more than twenty Panchayati union chair-persons, one district Panchayati president, more than hundred Gram Panchayat presidents and several thousands ward members are working in various bodies to look after the affairs of the people. A geographical location is represented by ward members, vice-president and president in village Panchayati council. Again the place is being represented by ward member, vice-president, president of District Panchayats. MLA and MP are also representing the same geographical location. Each and every layer of the bodies from village Panchayat to national parliament has its own role and function to be performed. MLA and MP have got earmarked money a crore and twenty-five lakh rupees respectively from the fund allocated for rural development activities. As per the specification of the schemes the representatives can spend the money. While spending the money it is all the more important to assess the issues and problems of the people and analyse the acuteness of the problems of the people and allocate money accordingly. To utilise the money a plan has to be chalked out through district planning committee. This process will help the representatives of the people to acquaint himself or herself with the problems of the people and by which they can effectively participate in the decision making process and likewise the representatives can act as animators to educate the people in the process of development.

10

FUNCTIONING OF GRAM PANCHAYAT AND GRAM SABHA IN TAMIL NADU

Introduction

New Panchayati Raj System in Tamil Nadu is to be visualised from the conflicting perceptions of bureaucracy, MPs and MLAs. There are three important major functions assigned to the grass-root level institutions namely participation of the people in the process of development at all levels, administering economic development and establishing equity among the social collectivities or administering social justice. The realisation of the basic objectives would be possible only when the provincial acts are enacted in consonance with the framework of the 73rd Amendment to the Constitution of India, the implementation of the provincial acts with the determined will of the leader, the increasing capacity of the local body leaders, changing attitude of the officials and the mobilization of the people towards the new dispensation of administering development. In Tamil Nadu, elections have been conducted, leaders have been positioned and yet adequate powers have not been devolved and as a result there is a continuous demand from the elected leaders for more powers and more resources to local bodies to meet the basic needs of the people in the rural areas.

The Problem

Are the Gram Panchayat and Gram Sabha functioning in line with the spirit of the decentralization of power or small government approach or good governance? Are the presidents of Gram Panchayats and members of Gram Sabha aware of their role and responsibilities to be discharged in the Panchayati System? Are the officials who work for administering development in the rural areas in the offices above the level of village Panchayats and the functionaries working within the jurisdiction of the Gram Panchayats cooperate with the elected leaders for the functioning of the local bodies? Do the leaders at the state level have the requisite will to implement the act with the sense of commitment and faith in Panchayats? Are the MPs and MLAs viewing the local bodies as complements and supplements to their functioning or threat to their political existence? Do the leaders of Local Bodies find enough intellectual support to gain momentum to discharge their duties? Have the elected leaders equipped themselves in building up their capacity to enhance their activities and tackle the problems of the rural populace? These are some of the vital questions to be probed into from the experience of Tamil Nadu.

Examination of the Cases

Gram Sabha is a basic unit which gives meaning to the concept participatory democracy or participation of people directly in the development process of the community in all the three levels namely decision making, implementing the same and in the evaluation process also. Role and function of Gram Sabha have been clearly explained in the act of the Tamil Nadu and yet it is dormant in its functioning as it has not been notified by the government so far. Neither the government nor the elected leaders of local bodies have real intention to keep this institution alive because it brings transparency and gives power to question the leadership while approving the decisions, money allocations, expenditure statement and annual report. Till date in Tamil Nadu the provision of Gram Sabha has not been invoked for its functioning as the reasons are known to all obviously. Arguments are always on the negative for Gram Sabha as it exceeds the manageable capacity of the local leaders due to the conflicting trends that prevail in the villages based on caste or party. Government has also set aside this provision without notifying it properly for a long period. Even though the beneficiary for all government schemes and programmes have to be identified only through Gram Sabha, the presidents are presenting the list of beneficiaries to the Block Panchayati office not in consultation with the Gram Sabha. Yet the list is being operated and sanctions have been accorded to them. It is an irony that none of the members of Gram Sabha raised questions objectively over the neglect of Gram Sabha by the elected village Panchayat presidents. But some of the NGOs are trying in the villages where they are working to convene the Gram Sabha by convincing the presidents with an aim of selecting beneficiaries for their programmes. Moreover there is an argument among the elected presidents of Gram Panchayats that if Gram Sabha is convened to take decisions, people, who have supported the defeated candidates in the election will oppose every move and act of the village Panchayat president. Yet another argument of the bureaucracy is that the convening of Gram Sabha is equivalent to the sleeping demon which will work against the existing order of the state. Hence they refuse and are reluctant to mobilise the people for Gram Sabha meetings.

Barring a few intellectuals, almost all are reluctant to support the proposal of convening of Gram Sabha to give life to a provision of the act. Gandhigram Rural Institute is planning to do it in the service villages while conducting PRA to prepare micro level plan. This can be documented and the same could be demonstrated to others that it is possible to conduct Gram Sabha.

Gram Panchayat leaders are slowly getting into the mill without proper training and orientation. After the election, the elected Panchayati presidents with a hope to bring schemes and programmes to the villages went to the Block Panchayat office and to their surprise, the officials did not respond to any of their demand. Presidents started meeting the Panchayat union chair-person to redress the grievances of the people of their villages. All their attempts to get things done in the Block Panchayat office are in vain. In the meanwhile everywhere there were tussles between the Panchayati union councillors and the presidents of the village Panchayats over sharing of powers and responsibilities. Panchayati union chair-persons have also taken a decision to support their councillors as they have been elected by the councillors and moreover the village Panchayati presidents are not in the Panchayati union councils. It went even to the level of passing a resolution in a Panchayati union council that the village Panchayati presidents should not come to the office premises of the Panchayati union. They were almost orphans in the Panchayati union office. This has been reported in the press.

In the meanwhile the Government of Tamil Nadu appointed a committee under the chairmanship of L.C. Jain to make recommendations to devolve powers to the three tiers of the Panchayati bodies. After seeing the acrimonious situation, the committee submitted its preliminary report and on the basis of the report a G.O. was issued in the month of October 1996. It was stated that nine poverty alleviation programme have to be executed by the village president himself. Prior of the G.O., there were some Gram Panchayati Presidents who have pressurised the Block Development Officer to get some contract work and by which they were caught into the corrupt net of the Block Development Office. There was no uniform procedure adopted throughout the state with regard to the functions of Gram Panchayats till the release of the new G.O. in the month of October 1996. It is another interesting feature that the G.O. issued in the month of October has not reached the persons concerned even after five months. After issuing this G.O., so far twelve Government orders have been issued in this connection. All these papers have not been circulated to the presidents of Gram Panchayats.

The officials have issued thirty-seven small booklets relating to the job of the president of the Gram Panchayats. Village Panchayat president has to operate three bank accounts for the three categories of the works. Panchayat president can spend up to Rs. 1000 for some maintenance work with the permission of the Panchayati councils through a resolution. All other expenditures exceeded Rs 1000 will have to go to Panchayati union office for getting sanction. Mostly the Panchayat presidents have to submit proposals to the Panchayati union and DRDA to get funds to implement schemes and programmes. All these programmes and schemes implemented by the Panchayats will be supervised by the officials.

Beneficiary selection brings a lot of conflicts among party men in the villages. They look at the issues from the party angle. In the selection process, all types of representatives namely MLA, MP, Panchayati Union Chair-person, District Panchayati president interfere and exert pressure on the president of Gram Panchayats.

Whenever centrally sponsored and state schemes are announced and money is being allocated, village Panchayat presidents have to submit proposal and get sanction from the Panchayati union office. In all the Panchayati union operated schemes, Panchayati union councillors interfered. As per the total allocation, sixty-five per cent has to go to the Gram Panchayats, twenty-five per cent should go to Panchayat unions and ten per cent should go to District Panchayats. All these allocations have to be utilised as per the stipulation of the governments both federal and provincial. On an average Rs. 1 lakh can be operated by a panchayat in this present arrangement. Now the commons can yield only Rs. 10,000 to the Panchayats. Most of the occasions oral instructions have been given to presidents to carry out certain programmes against norms. The presidents are in the hands of the MPs and MLAs.

Primary schools, health centres are supposed to be under the control of the Panchayats. In Tamil Nadu still it is with the State Government. Before the Government of Tamil Nadu makes announcement, the teachers and health workers preemptively demonstrated that they would be under the control of the State Government. They refused to work under Panchayats. Micro level planning is only in paper at the state level. It is not being practiced. Gram Sevak is a field worker who has been in the Panchayat since the origin of the post, has been taken away from the Panchayats and placed him/her in the Panchayati Union Office.

Corruption is another phenomenon shaking the very foundation of grass-root institutions. People who have spent money for their election have to get back their money by any means. Gram Panchayat Presidents, even in the available means, can get money from the beneficiaries. Presidents, who have indulged in corrupt practices have been caught by the people. The Gram Panchayats Presidents who are corrupt have to yield to the pressure of the officials.

At present, after hearing the arguments of the Union Finance Minister, opposition leader in the State Legislative Assembly and former member of State Planning Commission L.C. Jain, Chief Minister has agreed to constitute a committee of MLAs nominated by the respective political party, to go into the details of the functioning of Local Bodies and to make suggestions. Another interesting development takes place in Tamil Nadu that some of the intellectuals have joined together voluntarily to help the MLAs Committee to make recommendations and suggestions to improve the functioning of the Local Bodies.

Inferences

Panchayati institutions have been considered as only an implementing agency till today in Tamil Nadu from the perspective of the MPs and MLAs and state level political leaders. The local body leaders have not enhanced their capacity to manage these institutions. Gram Sabha has been relegated to the background though it has earmarked responsibilities. Local body leaders should have development orientation but in Tamil Nadu they have only political orientation. Administrative and accounting procedures are so complicated at their level of understanding and educational background. Too much of interference in the activities of panchayats by the MLAs, MPs and ministers directly and indirectly.

At all levels political parties are supporting the leaders at the grass-root level. But Gram Panchayats Presidents do not have political support as they have contested on a non-party basis since Gram Panchayats were freed from the clutches of the political parties. All development schemes and programmes are to be implemented only after getting sanction by submitting project proposal to Panchayati union office. The flow of funds from the state and federal governments has given an impression to the people that it is only an implementing agency of the programmes and schemes of the both governments. Very little scope is available for mobilising the resources from the common properties as they have been distributed to many. To get back all those commons Panchayat needs the support of Revenue Department. To enrich the common properties the local body leaders need adequate training. Training aspect has not been considered seriously by the State Government. State Planning Commission has submitted its recommendation with training module. State Institute of Rural Development (SIRD) has to be awakened from deep slumber and it has to be activated to meet the training need of at least officials and to some extent District Panchayat Presidents and Panchayat Union Chair-persons. Totally every year even in a small block Panchayat roughly one crore rupees are being spent on various programmes. Yet little impact is seen as leakages are abundant. Corruption has taken a very strong root and percolated into every aspect of life, village presidents have to face several ordeals as they are closer to the people and communities. Government is eating away its rules and orders without respecting them. There is a provision in the act for convening of Gram Sabha, but it is not being seriously viewed by the government when the Gram Panchayati Presidents have not convened the meeting. Even though order has been passed, the presidents have not convened the meeting of Gram Sabha. The Gram Panchayat Presidents' negative attitude towards Gram Sabha has been used by the officials, MPs and MLAs to threaten them.

Thus this power shift has its own problems. The problems and difficulties could be overcome by the involvement of the people. The Local Body leaders should have the ability to mobilise the people. By the transparent action, over a period of time good leadership will emerge at the grass-root level.

Areas for Immediate Investigation

The cumbersome administrative and accounting procedures have to be examined and suitable devices could be suggested. Organic linkages between and among the three tiers have to be studied. Need of the local body leaders has to be assessed. Conditions of the commons have to be investigated. Yet another important aspect resource mobilization could be explored with an objective of suggesting an alternative pattern. Perception of the MPs, MLAs and state level leaders towards the panchayati raj system has to be analysed. Large number of case studies have to be conducted. Impediments for the functioning of women and *dalit* leaders in discharging their responsibilities have to be seriously analysed. Functioning of Gram Sabha has to be carefully analysed and ways and means have to be suggested to strengthen the Gram Sabha. Suitable mechanism has to be devised to contain corruption at the grass-root level by doing continuous exercise. How the concept transparency works at the local bodies? has to be seen and suggest ways to make it mandatory to avoid corruption. Non-party basis Panchayat has to be reviewed in the light of the functioning of Gram Panchayats in Tamil Nadu.

Conclusion

Local bodies have been positioned to discharge the earmarked responsibilities. Yet, to fulfil the responsibilities, an array of steps have to be taken by the federal government and state government. Gram Sabha and Gram Panchayats are the foundations of the edifice of Indian Democracy. Functioning of Gram Sabha and Gram Panchayats in the context of varied perceptions of MLAs, MPs, bureaucracy and state level leaders warrants a thorough analysis to put them in proper place and shape in the light of the spirit of the 73rd Amendment to the Constitution of India. Management formula of Panchayati institutions has to be evolved more precisely to suit the needs of the local conditions. Capacity building exercise is the need of the hour for local body leaders.

11

FUNCTIONING OF BLOCK PANCHAYAT : A CASE ANALYSIS OF ATHOOR

ABDO - (Schemes)
CRSP
Jeevandhara
IRDP
65% of JVVT work in village panchayat
Power pumps
Hand pumps
Street lights

The ABDO is not having power to operate accounts. He is the supervisory cadre, inspecting all the accounts/registers, once in a month and send the report to the development officer (Panchayat) administration. Extension Officer for Panchayats is also inspecting the village Panchayats and giving necessary guidance to the village Panchayat president. All works above Rs. 5,000 should be estimated with the help of Union Engineer (Scheme). The 'M' book has to be countersigned by the ABDO and then only the village Panchayat president can withdraw the amount from the bank after resolution passed in the village Panchayat meeting.

The major role of ABDO and his staff is to streamline the accounts procedure and village

Panchayat administration in general.

The ABDO has written the comments on the records/account book itself, instructing to classify or rectify and report the same to him. By this arrangement, every month the village Panchayat income and expenditure is verified and properly monitored. This is an effective system compared to earlier procedure, the ABDO claimed.

During the monthly meeting, the Panchayat clerk is asked to bring all records. Occasionally the Panchayat presidents are also called to attend the meeting. The Panchayat clerk of Athoor Village Panchayat is a B.Com graduate. During the interview, he felt that the monthly meeting called by ABDO was more less a police investigation work; the officials do not frankly come forward to help the clerk or president. Their intention is to control and clutch the Panchayat affairs, the Panchayat clerk told.

The Plight of Panchayat Clerk

The Panchayat clerk is the administrative staff, in charge of the maintenance of all registers and record of the village Panchayats.

Salary of the clerk is fixed according to the total population of the village Panchayat. The minimum is Rs. 350 per month. Upto 6000 population it can be fixed upto Rs. 450. If the population is more than 6000 it can be fixed at Rs. 550. There are "old system Panchayat clerk" who are receiving Rs. 950 per month.

The new clerks who also have the same responsibilities as that of old clerk, receive only maximum of Rs. 550 per month as salary, whereas all old clerks receive Rs. 950 per month.

Regular BDO

The following schemes are under the control of regular BDO:

EAS
DDP
MPADS
Anna Marumalarchi
Namakku Name
10th Finance Union Share
General Fund
10th Finance Dist. Panchayat Share allotted works

1997-98 Expenditure Details

I.	10th Finance Commission -	
	allocation union share receiver	Rs. 6.40 lakhs
	District Panchayat allocated work	Rs. 4.10 lakhs
II.	JVVT Panchayat Union share	Rs. 8.32 lakhs
	DRDA share work	Rs. 13.96 lakhs
III.	DDP works allocated	Rs. 8.55 lakhs
IV.	Drought relief 2.60 + additional 3.50	Rs. 6.10 lakhs

Regular BDO/Staff Details

E.O. Social Welfare	1	
E.O. Small Savings	1	
Union Engineer	1	
Overseer	1	
Junior Assistants	5	
Accountant	1	
Office Manager	2	Administration - 1 Noon meal scheme - 1
Office Assistant	2	
Jeep Driver	1	

ABDO — Athoor Panchayat Union

I.	65% JVVT work in 22 village panchayats	Rs. 34.567 lakhs
II.	Group house (145 Nos.)	Rs. 39.15 lakhs
III.	Jeevandhara wells (27 Nos.)	Rs. 11.34 lakhs
IV.	CRSP (80 Nos.)	Rs. 1.60 lakhs
V.	IRDP (560 Nos.)	Rs. 19.56 lakhs
VI.	TRYSEM (24 beneficiaries)	
	Tailoring	- 10
	Typewriting	- 6
	Handicrafts	- 3
	Two wheeler mechanism	- 3
	Diesel Engine mechanism	- 2
		24

TABLE 11.1 : **Expenditure incurred from 1.4.97 to 31.12.97**

Sl. No.	Items	Amount in Rs.
1.	Current bill	2,647
2.	Current bill	49,395
3.	Salary	66,345
4.	Sitting allowance	2,575
5.	Stationery	1,342
6.	Streetlight maintenance	11,895
7.	T.V. maintenance	1,550
8.	Uniform to sweepers	8,076
9.	Funeral grant	1,400
10.	Deepavali advance	3,400
11.	Miscellaneous	12,343
12.	Road maintenance	16,982
13.	Drainage construction	3,44,430
14.	New pipe connection	33,798
15.	Furnitures at Panchayat Office	5,400
	Total	5,61,577

Source: Computed.

Ambathurai Village Panchayat
A Case Study on Income/Expenditure

TABLE 11.2 : **Total population hamlet-wise**

Sl. No.	Name	Men	Women	Total
1.	Ambathurai	997	1024	2021
2.	Muruganpatti	286	266	552
3.	Rengasamypuram	136	122	258
4.	Perumalkoilpatti	1268	1270	2538
5.	Kollapatti	208	213	421
6.	Indirapuram	168	167	335
7.	Kathirpatti	88	89	177
8.	Kurumbapatti	247	263	510
9.	Nadupatti	220	223	443
10.	Ramanathapuram	443	443	886
11.	Velampatti	13	12	25
	Total	4074	4092	8166

Water Sources

Hand pump total - 31 Nos.
Pipe (Street/public) - 106 Nos.

Schools

CSI Primary	-	2
Adi Dravidar High School	-	1
Adi Dravidar Primary	-	1
Union Primary	-	4
Noon meal centre	-	8
Noon meal centre with school	-	8
Total Street lights	-	132

Grant received for the year 1997-98

I. 10th Finance Commission quarterly allocation Rs. 84,623

	For the year Rs. 84,623 × 4	Rs. 3,38,492
II.	65% JVVT allocation (two quarters received) Rs. 81,800 × 4	Rs. 3,27,200
III.	Earmarked fund	Rs. 45,000
	Total	Rs. 7,10,692

TABLE 11. 3 : **JVVT Works carried out in Details**

S.No.	Place	Type of work	Amount in Rs.
1.	Ramanathapuram	Retaining wall	12,757
2.	Kathirpatti	Retaining wall	5,968
3.	Perumalkoilpatti	Retaining wall	15,225
4.	Ambathurai	Small bridge	10,968
5.	Muruganpatti	Culvert	12,440

TABLE 11.4 : **Statement of Income and Expenditure for 1996-97**

Income		Expenditure	
L.C. Patta	1,630	8 OHT operator salary	13,760
Stamp duty	30,452	3 Sweepers salary	5,430
Interest	3,075	Panchayat clerk TA	1,479
Professional tax	12,732	St. light maintenance	4,615
House tax (collected)	8,000	Current bill	26,634
Building license	12,719	Water supply	8,712
Funeral grant	1,600	Miscellaneous	1,421
Street light maintenance Govt. grant	1,327	Funeral grant	3,000
		Celebration	50
	71,444		65,071
Opening balance	4,349	Cash at hand	10,722
	75,793		75,793

TABLE 11.5 : **Budget Estimate for 1998-99 (Expenditure)**

Sl.No.	Items of expenditure	Amount in Rs.
1.	Salary	60,500
2.	T.A	9.000
3.	Stationery	12,000
4.	Current bill street lights	21,000
5.	Current bill OHT	26,500
6.	Current bill Buildings	15,200
7.	Well maintenance	10,000
8.	Hand pump maintenance	10,000
9.	Water supply maintenance	40,000
10.	Street lights maintenance	27,500
11.	Tank maintenance	13,000
12.	Celebration	3,500
13.	Panchayat office maintenance	5,000
14.	Equipments maintenance	1,000
15.	Road/Small bridges maintenance	22,000
16.	Library repayment	3,000
17.	Fixed deposit return	2,500
18.	Advances	4,000
19.	New building	10,000
20.	New road/bridges	10,000
21.	Street light extension	55,000
22.	Water tap extension	10,000
23.	Water tap maintenance	20,000
24.	New road	10,000

Source: Computed.

TABLE 11.6 : **Expected Receipts for the year 1998-99**

Sl. No.	Sources	Amount in Rs.
1.	House tax	27,500
2.	Library	2,700
3.	Professional tax	20,000
4.	Miscellaneous	2,500
5.	License fee	1,500
6.	Building license	2,000
7.	Interest	3,500
8.	Tree auction	500
9.	Local cess	2,000
10.	Local cess surcharge	1,500
11.	Government allocation	3,40,000
12.	Deposit	1,500
13.	Funeral grant	2,500
14.	Matching grant (House tax)	26,500
		4,34,700
	Cash at bank	23,000
		4,57,700

Source: Computed.

12

FUNCTIONING OF DISTRICT PANCHAYAT: A CASE ANALYSIS OF DINDIGUL

District Panchayat has come to limelight only after receiving the communication from the Directorate of Rural Development on 17th February, 1997. It gives guidelines for District Panchayat with regard to 10th Finance Commission allocation of grants. It underlines the fact that the works under the grant can be selected by the district Panchayat whereas the implementation must be by the concerned department of the government through the Panchayati union and Gram Panchayat. They should be allotted through tender. Concerned department will perform this task and the District Panchayat should not call for tenders and decide.

As per the G.O. No. 227 of 3.3.97, the district collector sanctioned Rs. 64 lakhs for the activities of the District Panchayat from Rs. 1 crore sanctioned by the Government of Tamil Nadu to each district. They have sanctioned Rs. 20 lakhs for administrative expenses. Of the Rs. 64 lakhs allotted for the activities, 20% of the amount can be spent on street lights and 80% of the amount can be spent for other necessary works. Amount should not be utilised for the works completed earlier. The amount can be spent only for new works. Works can be selected in consultation with the district ward members and Block

Development Officer. The estimate for all those works must be sanctioned with the approval of the technical division. For all the works, material available in Panchayat union can be purchased by cheque payment.

The Chief Executive Officer of District Panchayat has sent a communication to all block development officers on 27th March 1997 informing the allocation of ten lakh rupees to each union as per the allocation of 10th Finance Commission recommendation. Here it is also informed that priority of works have to be indicated for immediate sanction and implementation. Drinking water supply is spelt out in the priority list.

Yet another circular from Directorate of Rural Development, Government of Tamil Nadu informs the role and functions of the three tiers of the Tamil Nadu Panchayati system as per the direction of G.O. No. 75 (R.D.C.) dated 14th March 1997. As per the circular with regard to central government schemes.

a. District Panchayat has only a planning-cum-advisory role;
b. Block Panchayat and Gram Panchayat are implementing agencies;
c. Gram Panchayat has power to select and implement individual beneficiaries oriented programmes;
d. Block Panchayat office has to provide necessary technical and other assistance to village Panchayat.

The schemes referred here are: IRDP, CRSP, TRYSEM, MES, JVVT, IAY, EAS.

District Panchayat president has sent a request for installation of AC machine in the office of the District Panchayat. On 17th March, 1997 a circular was issued to all collectors, Chief Executive Officers informing them that there is no such provision for installation of AC plant. Likewise, a ceiling limit on the fuel consumption for the vehicle allotted to District Panchayat has been fixed per month as follows:

Petrol 195 litres.

Diesel 125 litres.

Panchayati institutions leaders have demanded perks and facilities for them since their inception. On 27th March 1997 a G.O. No. 101 was issued in connection with the fixation of TA and sitting allowances to leaders and members of local bodies. The details are given below:

TABLE 12.1 : **Details of Allowances to Local Body Members**

Sl. No.	Category	Travel	D.A. (Rs.)	Sitting Allowance (Rs.)
1.	District panchayat president/members	I class	50	100
2.	Block panchayat chairman	I class	30	75
3.	Block panchayat councillors	II class	20	50
4.	Gram panchayat president	I class	20	50
5.	Gram panchayat ward members	II class	—	25

Source: Computed.

Yet another circular was issued to all collectors from the Directorate of Rural Development. This circular explains the revision of the existing accounting procedures of village Panchayat account. There are three accounts to be maintained in each village panchayat namely: a) Village Panchayat fund account; b) Village Panchayat earmarked account; c) Village Panchayat scheme fund account. Accounts should not be in the personal name of the president.

The accounts should be operated jointly by the president and vice-president. Exception is also provided, if there is any adverse relationship between the President and the vice-president, the village Panchayat members can nominate any one of the members to operate the account jointly with the president. But it has to be approved by the district collector. This new circular instructs that the balance amount of each village Panchayat should be in Local Fund II to village panchayat Fund Account before 30th April.

G.O. No. 92 dated 20th March 1997 supplies details regarding rationalisation of village Panchayat accounts by providing 31 set of village Panchayat forms. It is also mentioned that the Block Development Officer/Panchayat union commissioner confines himself to Panchayat union activities and implementation of noon meal programme, small savings, social welfare schemes, eye camps and execution of works entrusted to Panchayat union under the schemes of decentralised district planning, MLA and MP area development schemes.

Yet another communication from Directorate of Rural Development to district Collector dated 11th April, 1997 informed that the Extension Officer is redesignated as Deputy BDO (Panchayats). Panchayat Assistant is responsible for collection and remittance of dues and maintenance of the various registers. A separate circular from the Directorate of Rural Development informs that Rs. 3640 is the estimated cost towards the installation of one street light.

Further communication was received from the Secretary, Rural Development regarding the circular sent by the Government of India, Ministry of Rural Areas & Employment in connection with the participation of women members in the local body institutions. To ensure effective participation of women in the functioning of local body institutions, steps have to be taken. Proxy has to be avoided. Another D.O. letter No. 15177 dated 9th April, 1997 requesting officials to avoid discouragement of women and SC members participation while they perform their roles and function.

For district Panchayat meeting, circular will be sent by the Chief Executive Officer to all the members of the council. District Panchayat meeting was held on 20th October 1996, 23rd Dec. 1996, 12th February 1997, 10th April 1997, 14th May 1997, 15th July 1997, 19th August 1997, and 14th September 1997. The following official representatives from the Government Departments and autonomous institutions have attended the meeting:

1. Chief Education Officer;
2. PWD Executive Engineer;
3. TWARD Executive Engineer;
4. Deputy Director of Animal Husbandry;
5. District SC Welfare Officer;
6. District BC/MBC Welfare Officer;
7. TNEB Assistant Engineer;
8. Personal Assistant to Collector for Panchayat Development;
9. District Development Officer Divisional;
10. Joint Registrar of Cooperatives; and
11. District Rural Development Agency Project Officer.

In this meeting schemes and financial allocation of the concerned departments have been explained. Further it was decided to bring out a book containing all information relating to schemes and programmes of the government.

There is another communication from the District Collector to district Panchayat president about the financial allocation under decentralised district plan preparation and approval. It is informed that Rs. 103.31 lakh have been earmarked for Dindigul district. Government order No. 173 dated 23rd June 1997 directs the administration to include district Panchayat in the district level consumer protection council.

Further the Government Order No. 235 dated 22nd July, 1997 informs the allocation of funds to district Panchayats based on the budget estimate of the year 1997-98. Total allocation is Rs. 30.95 crores. Of the total allocation of Rs. 30.95 crores Government releases Rs. 7.74 crores to District Panchayat as first instalment. From this allocation, Dindigul district gets the amount of Rs. 27,87,563.

By the circular of the Directorate of Rural Development the district president can directly release the money to the Gram Panchayat presidents for IRDP scheme. JVVT fund has to be allocated as per the following ration:

65% of the total allocation should be sent to Gram Panchayats.

15% of the total allocation should be sent to Panchayati Union.

20% of the total allocation should be sent to District Panchayats.

District Collector is authorised to select villages for Indira Avas Yojana scheme of housing construction. In this scheme fund will be released to village Panchayat directly. Again collector is authorised to allocate number of wells to Panchayat union and Panchayats. They are responsible for selecting beneficiaries and implementation of the programme also.

Employment assurance schemes are to be implemented by Agricultural Engineering Department, PWD, Panchayat Union. There is no role of Gram Panchayat in this scheme. Under EAS scheme the following category of works could be undertaken:

Category I : Percolation ponds, small tanks, village tanks, temple ponds, irrigation channels and soil conservation.

Category II : Link roads, small bridges, retention walls.

Category III : Community assets, schools, balwadi, creche and public distribution centres.

List of Departments functioning in the District

1. Revenue Department - DRO
2. Backward Class and Minority Welfare
3. Personal Assistant to Collector for Panchayat Development
4. Assistant Executive Engineer (Hand Pump Maintenance)
5. District Education Office
6. Lead Bank Officer
7. TWARD
8. Forest Department
9. Road Transport Office
10. Deputy Registrar (Milk Society)
11. Joint Director Medical and Family Welfare
12. Divisional Engineer (Highway Division)
13. Executive Engineer (Western Ghat Development Scheme)
14. Deputy Director (Health)
15. Regional Joint Director (Animal Husbandry)
16. Chief Executive Officer (Fishermen Development Council)
17. Superintendent Engineer (Fishery)
18. Deputy Director (Horticulture)
19. Special Deputy Tahsildar (Public grievance redressal)
20. District Coordinator (Arivoli Iyakkam)
21. District Civil Supply Officer

22. Joint Registrar (Cooperative Societies)
23. Inspector (Women Schools)
24. District Town Panchayat Joint Director
25. Information and Public Relation Officer
26. Sidha Medicine - Official
27. Municipal Commissioner
28. THADCO Manager
29. PWD Executive Engineer
30. Social Welfare Officer
31. Adi Dravida Welfare Officer
32. Joint Director Agriculture
33. Divisional Development Officer
34. Joint Director Handloom and Spinning
35. DIC General Manager
36. Managing Director of Transport Corporation
37. Chief Educational Officer
38. District Rural Development Agency
39. Assistant. Director Khadi and Village Industries
40. District Employment Officer

Series of communications have been received by the local bodies from the state government. They are given in Table 12.2.

TABLE 12.2 : **List of Government Orders with Details**

Sl. No.	G.O.No.	Date	Subject
1.	92	26-3-97	Account rationalisation
2.	93	26-3-97	Details of grants withheld
3.	101	27-3-97	T.A. to Panchayat leaders
4.	186	10-6-97	Additional typist to Panchayat Union
5.	167	10-6-97	Additional Assistant to Panchayat Union
6.	188	10-6-97	Promotion of Record Assistant to Record Clerk
7.	189	10-6-97	Typist/Assistant job exchange
8.	191	10-6-97	Mercy ground employment
9.	192	10-6-97	Enhancement of salary to Panchayat Clerk
10.	202 203 204 205	16-7-97	Rearrangement of APOs
11.	225	16-7-97	Informing district-wise dealers streetlight spares/ bulb purchase
12.	244	1-8-97	Reorganisation of administrative set-up

13

STATE SPONSORED SCHEMES IN TAMIL NADU

Introduction

Political leaders and parties have been adopting certain strategies to hold back the mass under their sway continuously to stay in power. The strategies range from evolving slogans to adopting innovative policies which attract the mass for some time. Staying in power depends upon the strategy and the capacity of the leader and the party to attract the mass. There is no permanent strategy to attract the mass. Hence parties and leaders have to change the strategy from time to time. Leaders are taking care in evolving strategies to draw the attention of the people. All the leaders cannot be successful in all the times. It is just like a game. In the context of fast changing socio-economic and political scenario, leaders are to be more sensitive in understanding the pulse of the people and they are to be so innovative in evolving strategy. In the fifty years of democratic governance, leaders have adopted several strategies to hold the mass under their sway. Certain strategies have yielded good results and certain strategies have not yielded any result to the tune of their expectation. From Indian National Congress to the Dravida Munnetra Kazhagam parties both national and regional have adopted several strategies to woo the voters. The strategy may vary in its nature. It may be a mere slogan or a policy option or a course of action. "Do or die" of Indian National Congress during the freedom struggle held the people together under the leadership of Mahatma Gandhi. "Alleviate Poverty" helped Mrs. Indira Gandhi to stay back in power for some time through her policy options such as abolition of privy purse, nationalization of banks and introduction of twenty-point programme. "Save democracy" helped Janata party to come to power. Establishing stable government to save India helped Indira Gandhi to come back to power. Eradication of corruption in public life helped the National Front to come to power by defeating the Indian National Congress. Likewise certain leaders stayed back in power due to their policy options. Jyoti Basu is in power for more than two decades due to his several revolutionary policy options and especially due to empowerment of people through grass-root democracy. Dravidian parties have been in power one after another through their welfare policy options. Now the DMK is in power. It is striving to keep the mass under its fold. Hence it introduced two new programmes namely Anna Marumalarchi Thittam and Nammakku Naame Thittam. These two programmes are oriented towards the development of the rural areas with an objective of drawing the people of the rural areas towards the DMK. Validity and implication of the programme is gauged on the basis of its delivery not on the basis of its components. It is more important to what extent it attracts the mass by extending its services. For example the noon meal scheme of M.G. Ramachandran had an everlasting implication on the mass.

DMK tries its level best to give an innovative programme as given by Kerala government through its mass campaign approach for people's planning,

Andhra Pradesh government through its Janmabhoomi programme, West Bengal government through its land reform and Panchayati system. Of the programmes, Kerala and West Bengal programmes are bringing name to the government and the leaders as these programmes go through the people's organisation and the involvement of the officials are always on supportive basis. DMK government conceived it as an innovative programme and for that matter no programme from West Bengal to Kerala including Janmabhoomi programme is new and innovative. All are advocated and practiced by the Father of our Nation in India at the dawn of Independence.

The Indian political parties have tried their options but they could not achieve success enduringly and hence now shamelessly switching over to Gandhian model or framework of development without using his nomenclature by giving different names to attract the mass. Even in performing this task, they could have perfected the programme in such a fashion to bring sustainable development. China followed the Gandhian model and following the path of China, West Bengal and in the same way Kerala have started adopting it for development. The communists have admitted the fact that Gandhian model has solutions to the problems of the people and hence they evolved programmes with more pragmatic concern. But other parties have no such pragmatic concern and most of the programmes are so dogmatic that they face several problems when they are put into practice.

To understand the new programmes of the DMK government for rural development and their implications this exercise is undertaken. What are the objectives of the new programmes such as Anna Marumalarchi Thittam and Nammakku Naame Thittam? What practical implications in the rural society they have got? How they are being implemented in the villages? are major thrust of our discussion here. The two schemes have more or less the same objectives. They are:

a. The basic needs of the rural areas have to be fulfilled within a short span of time.
b. The programmes have to be introduced in a selective manner in the selected villages and not in all villages of Tamil Nadu.
c. To bring the marginalised weaker sections under this fold to make them to participate in the development process. Enough service components should be included in these programmes to help this sector.
d. Operationally the two schemes are having different characteristics.

To provide basic facilities to all sections of the society they have been conceived. It is nothing new and the schemes of rural development have to be integrated and to be implemented in the selected villages so as to enable the Panchayat to develop the economy and to administer social justice. In each assembly constituency a single village will be selected based on the population and that Gram Panchayat should be a very big one. Seven facilities are indicated under this scheme:

1. Drinking water supply
2. Primary education
3. Public health
4. Nutrition programme
5. Housing
6. Rural roads
7. Fair price shops

Drinking Water Supply

All citizens of the Panchayat will get adequate water

supply. Each individual will get forty litres of water.

Education

Basic facilities including building of primary schools, drinking water supply, sanitation, maintenance of buildings should be provided under this scheme. Steps will be taken to provide education to all women students upto eighth standard. Achieving cent per cent literacy.

Health

Twenty-four hours hospital with all facilities has to be created in the particular village under this scheme. Anti-natal care, post-natal care, reproductive health, family welfare and awareness creation on AIDS are the activities of the hospital.

Nutrition Programme

Providing nutritive food to all the children in the village. For about thirty-six months from the birth special attention will be given to all the children.

Housing

Indira Avas scheme will be implemented in the village. Executing the single light schemes in the villages.

Rural Roads

All roads will be converted into metal and tar road. Facility could be created to draw the attention of the transport corporation.

Fair Price Shop

All villages of the Gram Panchayat will be provided with fair price shop.

Social Welfare

Muvaloor Ramamirtham scheme, Muthulakshmi Reddi scheme, pension to orphans, housing patta to landless, laying roads to cremation ground will be implemented in the village.

Economic Development

Loans could be arranged through cooperative societies for economic development activities. Training the village youth in small trade is yet another programme for the village. Generating employment opportunity for the villagers through the skill available in the villages.

Providing public reading room, telephone facility, post office, constructing T.V. room will be some other activities of the village under this scheme. Implementing total prohibition in the village, providing toilet facilities to all the houses in the village, and eradicating child labour in the village are some of the programmes. Tree planting will be encouraged. Each family should have a savings account under this scheme.

Anna Marumalarchi Thittam has the following characteristics:

a. All the development programmes have to be completed within a year.
b. Break-up programme is possible within one year. It can be three to six months programme or six to twelve months programme.

c. The selection of work is based on the joint decision of the chair-person of the block panchayat, Block Panchayat Commissioner and village Panchayat president.
d. The financial support is fully done by the state government.

Directions for Nammakku Naame Thittam

Gram Sabha has to be convened. Before convening the Gram Sabha, schemes have to be selected to meet the requirements of the village. Schemes have to be selected in such a fashion to get the share of the people for the activities. Quantum of human labour and money have to be decided. Whitewashing the building, repairing the roads, repairing the tanks and irrigation channels have to be selected and in all the activities, people have to be involved.

Nammakku Naame Thittam has the following characteristics:

a. No specific period is mentioned. It can be a long range scheme selected or evolved by the people.
b. It is a continuous programme and break up is not needed and not possible also.
c. The works and programmes are to be selected or evolved and approved by the people.
d. All the works are to be carried out only by the participation of people without wage. Three-fourth of expenditure will be met by the State government.

It is inferred from the basic objectives and characteristics of the two schemes that the development programmes are not having any new component but the schemes and programmes sponsored by the state and central government have been channelised and diverted to a particular selected village. It is mere concentration of schemes and programmes of rural development sponsored by the centre and the state under the direction of the district administration with the knowledge of the local body leaders.

To study the operation of Anna Marumalarchi Thittam, a study has been undertaken in a village where it is being implemented. It is a policy decision that each village of this scheme will get Rs. 110 lakhs for the coverage of all the programmes of work. This will be implemented in 234 villages of 234 assembly constituencies of Tamil Nadu. Silukkuvarpatti panchayat has been selected for this programme. Following schemes have been suggested under this scheme for this village:

a. To construct a drainage system in all the ten villages of the Silukkuvarpatti panchayat;
b. Providing adequate street lights in all the ten villages in this panchayat;
c. To construct group houses to SC and ST of the ten villages of this panchayat;
d. To construct a community hall in Silukkuvarpatti;
e. To ensure adequate water supply to all the ten villages through constructing overhead tanks and linking them with pipe lines.
f. To provide toilet facilities to all the ten villages to maintain water supply.

Likewise to study the Nammakku Naame Thittam, Veelinaickanpatti has been selected as the programme is being implemented in this Gram Panchayat.

Under this scheme the following programmes have been carried out:

a. White washing of school building;

b. road repair works have been completed;
c. desilting and deepening of tanks have been completed.

While going through the above discussed programmes one would infer that it is mere diluting of the sponsored schemes of both governments.

The schemes have not been implemented as they have been conceived. Government of Tamil Nadu has announced this scheme with all fanfare but to implement the scheme it has sanctioned only thirty-eight lakhs which is very meagre to meet the demands of the people. It is not going to be a successful scheme. This programme is based not on the needs of the village but it is based on the available scheme of the government at the hands of district administration.

Likewise Nammakku Naame scheme is a participatory programme and it is more voluntary in nature. At present voluntay work force from the village is only a lip service. Nobody would come forward to do this service as people have been oriented to expect anything from the Government. Hence to bring this scheme to the village what the president of Gram Panchayat and officials are doing is that budget is prepared in such a fashion to meet the voluntary labour force charge in the 75% of the allocation of the Government and by which this scheme brings a new kind of corruption in the development administration of the villages.

After the enactment of the 73rd Constitutional Amendment, schemes and programmes of the governments have to be reduced. But the state governments insists that more flexibility should be provided in the centrally sponsored schemes which they are being implemented in the rural areas of different states taking into account the regional and cultural variations of the states. Yet the state governments are proliferating more number of schemes which are contradictory to the concept of decentralization of power. Moreover the new schemes are not innovative. Some of them are repetitive. Both central and state governments are acting against the New Panchayati Raj System by proliferating schemes. When the federal government introduced the MP local area development scheme by allocating Rs. 1 crore, state government started introducing the MLA local area developmental scheme by giving Rs. 25 lakhs and by which executive works have been assigned to the MPs and MLAs. Now local bodies are under the influence of MPs, MLAs and elected local body leaders are in utter confusion rather than in clarity to achieve development.

14

AN AGENDA FOR IMMEDIATE ACTION

The 73rd Amendment to the Constitution of India is only a framework and a guideline which sets in motion the grass-root level legitimate institutions to perform certain specific roles. But the fundamental principle of the amendment is to make the Panchayati bodies as institutions of self-governance. There is no dispute over this basis. The problem arises only in the implementation process. The implementation process of the 73rd constitutional amendment begins in the formulation of the state act itself. The defects in the state act will completely cripple the functioning of the local bodies or it would produce a dependency syndrome among the Panchayati leaders. While seeing the provisions of the act, one should be conscious of the basic objective of the 73rd constitutional amendment and the preamble of the act of the province. The governing clause of the 73rd constitutional amendment act, 243(G) stresses the economic development and social justice. Thus working for economic development and administering equity starts from generating employment opportunities and the provisions of the act should enable the Panchayats to function in such a manner and for which the provincial act should have a major emphasis on economic development functions in the body of the act. The existing act of Tamil Nadu emphasis is on service functions as in the previous act. The present act has to be amended by incorporating the subjects shown "Functions of the Panchayats."

The organic linkages between the village Panchayats and the Panchayati union, Panchayati union and District Panchayats have to be maintained. Each one is a complementary to the other. The present trend of conflict with each other in the local bodies has to be avoided by eliminating the panchayati union and District Panchayat wards.

Participation of people in the development process is another key element of the new Panchayati Raj System. Gram Sabha is a body wherein all the people of a particular village can participate in the decision making, implementation and evaluation process. Today it seems that no Panchayati leader is coming forward to convene the Gram Sabha meeting as they have developed a jittery over the people. Even the officials are not bothered about the convening of Gram Sabha even though it is mandatory that it has to be convened at least twice a year and the gap should not exceed six months. Beneficiaries have to be selected only in Gram Sabha. Yet it is not being convened. The reasons are many. First in a multi-caste village, the Gram Sabha meeting will become a seed-bed for conflicts as it takes decision and makes allocation. Second the voters ranging from thousand to three thousand bring the question of manageability. Where it will be convened who will manage a crowd of thousand or thousand five hundred? Will it be possible to discuss anything in a big crowd? Thirdly the quorum. Quorum has to be fixed at the lowest level as participative culture of our people is very low. Even the powers of the Gram Sabha have to be modified. It is a body to prioritise the need and to select the beneficiaries of the government schemes.

Decision making powers should be vested with the council of Village Panchayat. But the council has to inform the Gram Sabha about the activities of the Panchayat periodically. Instead of the Gram Sabha, it must have either Ward Sabha or Hamlet Sabha as in Kerala and Orissa to ensure effective participation of the people in the development process of the community.

The existing arrangement of resource mobilization, proliferation of centrally sponsored schemes are always against the spirit of decentralization of power. Panchayats are not agents to implement the programmes of the provincial government and the central government. It has got its own original functions. It has to plan for an integrated development of the rural areas. Thus the local bodies should have control over the resources and should be given power to mobilize resources through tax and levy. To enable the Panchayati bodies to act as independent governing institutions the entire tax system has to be changed. Till then as in other states like Kerala and West Bengal 40 to 50 per cent of the resources should be earmarked for local bodies as untied funds with a stipulation that major portion of money should be utilised for productive functions like generating employment opportunities. Further to enable the Panchayats to have control over common property resources the revenue departments have given instructions to help the local bodies and if needed suitable legislation has to be enacted.

For the smooth and fair conduct of election, an Election Commission has to be constituted which will function independently. While appointing the Election Commissioner, tenure should be either five or six years. They should not be kept in tender hook to stick on to the office by getting extension in every two years. The existing provision of two-year tenure will certainly affect the freedom of the commission. It has to be amended in the act.

Members of Parliament and Members of Legislative Assembly are operating one crore and twenty-five lakhs of rupees respectively for area development programme. The very logic of the programme is wrong as Parliament and Legislative Assembly have earmarked responsibilities and well-defined functions and their entry in the local bodies through their programme weakens the local body institutions. Further in other provinces MPs and MLAs are not made members of the local bodies. But in Tamil Nadu they are coming in the local bodies with all their powers and it ultimately cripples the independence of the local bodies. All the programmes of MPs and MLAs are to be operated only through the local bodies. The allocation of rupees one crore and twenty-five lakhs to MPs and MLAs respectively gave hope to the local body leaders that they can also demand a quantum of money from the government and thus the entire local body system of governance will witness a topsy turvy change in due course. A suitable mechanism has to be evolved to integrate these quantum of money to tackle the local problems through the District Planning Committee (DPC). There should be very close coordination among the MPs, MLAs and local body leaders in utilising the area development scheme money.

Yet another important issue in Tamil Nadu in the functioning of local body institutions is the transfer of functionaries from the government of Tamil Nadu to local bodies. The effective functioning of agriculture, health and education department can be ensured only when accountability and transparency are maintained. To ensure transparency and accountability the functionaries of local bodies have to be transferred to local bodies. Government can maintain the records and retain the power of distributing their salaries. Other states have already transferred these officials to local bodies and they are working very well. Kerala is the best in transferring the officials to local bodies and ensuring the smooth functioning and that could be followed here also.

The role of the collector as inspector of Panchayats is wielding unlimited powers of control over the Panchayati bodies. The power of dismissal is being given to district collectors. Normally that power should be given only to the democratically elected bodies or a tribunal could be constituted to look into the complaints of the local body leaders. Best model could be borrowed from the state of Kerala in this regard. Micro level planning could be initiated and people could be trained in the art of planning for development at the micro level. Before we initiate the Tenth Plan proposal, people could be adequately involved in this planning in the Ninth Plan period itself. Suitable mechanism has to be evolved based on the report of the State Planning Commission.

Tamil Nadu has witnessed frequently caste conflicts and to avoid it steps could be taken at macro level but at the same time it could be tackled locally by constituting people committees in village Panchayats with the approval of Panchayats, and appropriately, at block level and district level this could also be created legitimately. This type of village committees work in West Bengal effectively.

A committee has to be constituted to identify the state laws which are impediments to implement the provisions of the new act and the same could be rectified by amending the same.

Panchayati Raj Act is not a piece of legislation alone. In our country there are symbolic legislations which have been enacted to claim that the government has had an act and beyond that it has no significant implication. Panchayat is not of that sorts. It is an alternative to the existing mechanism to rejuvenate grass-root democracy. It should be made as mass movement for social transformation and economic development. This could be done only with the active support of the state government. Will the Chief Minister play a decisive role in empowering people? Hence needed attention should be given by the state.

As Panchayati leaders have more responsibilities and functions and to discharge their role and responsibilities, their capacity has to be enhanced and managerial skill has to be increased. To enhance their capacity, training programmes have to be organised periodically and for which a permanent arrangement has to be evolved. Panchayati president, Panchayati union chair-person District Panchayati president and members of the three councils have to be provided with some monetary assistance depending upon their work load.

Steps to be taken in a nutshell

1. Changing the tenor of the act from service functions to original function of planning, implementation and evaluation of programmes to create employment, achieving economic development and equity.
2. District Panchayat president should be made the District planning committee president.
3. Officials working in Panchayati jurisdiction should be transferred to Panchayats retaining their pay and pension with state government. They are accountable only to the Panchayats.
4. The local community should be enabled to control the resources, especially the common property resources.
5. Unnecessary linkages on the present arrangement

of ward members of Panchayat Union and District Panchayats should be removed and in this place Gram Panchayat members and Panchayat Union chair-persons will be made as members of Panchayat Union and District Panchayats respectively.

6. To ensure real participation of the people in Gram Sabha meeting quorum has to be fixed at a lower level than that of the stipulation of today. New arrangement like Ward Sabha could be thought of. Moreover the powers of Gram Sabha have to be restricted while considering the existing local conditions. But it should be ensured that the Gram Sabha has to be convened as per the stipulation.
7. Sizeable reduction should be made in centrally sponsored schemes and programmes for rural development and untied funds should be increased to facilitate local bodies to evolve their own programmes.
8. Local area development scheme of MPs and MLAs is totally against the principle of decentralization of power. However, the present allocation of money has to be systematically integrated at the district level to avoid duplication and wastages,
9. 40% to 50% of total revenue should be earmarked for the rural development works through the local bodies.
10. To make the local bodies really a self governing institution, the entire tax system has to be studied and appropriate step has to be taken to devolve levying powers to local bodies to increase the resources of the local bodies.
11. Election Commission's independence has to be maintained and for which the period of the office of the Commissioner has to be fixed at least for five years.

12. Arbitrary powers of the district collector in dismissing the elected Panchayats is to be removed from the act. These types of decisions have to be taken by the next higher local body.
13. District Rural Development Agency must be put under the control of the District Panchayat or it can be abolished.
14. Steps should be taken to make this a people's movement. The best way is to initiate people's planning process. Steps have to be initiated for micro-level planning.
15. A committee should be constituted to identify the existing laws which are deterrent to the devolution of powers to the local bodies.
16. L.C. Jain committee recomendations have to be implemented.
17. Conflict Resolution Committees in the village, taluk and district level have to be constituted with the approval of the respective bodies.
18. Village vigilance committee has to be formed to perform the watchdog functions and inform the misdeeds if any to appropriate authorities.
19. Capacity-building exercise have to be conducted for local body leaders. Suitable machinery has to be evolved in this regard.
20. Suitable emoluments to local body leaders depending upon their work load has to be thought of.

15

CASE ANALYSIS OF GRAM PANCHAYATS

CASE-I : VADUGAMBADI

This gram panchayat is in Gujiliamparai panchayat union (Block) and it is earmarked for scheduled caste. Mr. Perumal son of a former Panchayat President contested in the election. He won the election. His grandfather was a ward member of the same panchayat and his father was a President of the same gram panchayat. He was also a ward member of the same panchayat in the previous period. Interestingly he got his education in a Gandhian Institution in Rural Development branch and joined in Communist Party of India (Marxist). His marriage with a Reddiar caste girl has enhanced his status as he conducted his marriage in a dignified way with the approval of his family and the family of the bride. His wife, a staff nurse worked in the same village for some time and earned a good name in the village by her dedicated service.

He has been oriented by his grandfather and father for social service activities. Further reinforcement was done by the Communist Party of India (Marxist). His wife has been transferred to Palani due to political reasons as he protested against some of the activities of the MLA of his constituency in the interest of the people. Now he is with his parents in the said village and he visits his wife only on Saturday and Sunday. He has two sons. His family has twelve acres of land and all the lands are cultivable in nature. His father is cultivating the lands.

From his early childhood he was drawn towards Communist Party of India as it appeared that it would work for the poors and labourers. Since this region is a dry belt which is not providing adequate employment opportunity, people are being exploited by the moneyed class. As people's problems have been addressed by the Communist Party of India (Marxist) in his area he was drawn towards this party though his father's lenience was towards the Dravida Munnetra Kazhagam. Despite his difference of opinion with his father he joined in the Communist Party of India (Marxist) and took part actively in politics. He was imprisoned many times when he joined with the party organisers to agitate against the exploitation of the agricultural labourers by the landlords and workers of the factories by the owners of the factories. He learnt the art of mobilising the people against any exploitation by any group through his party. It is his style of functioning from the beginning that he used to write petitions to government offices for benefits to individuals from the schemes of the government and successfully got benefits to individuals. This kind of activities had been carried out continuously in his village. He never anticipated this kind of institution is going to be installed for local governance. This draws the attention of all people towards him. He never distanced himself from other caste Hindu groups. He has been freely moving with other communities.

In the Gram Panchayat election five candidates have contested. Since this Gram Panchayat is reserved for SC, five candidates from SC community belonging to different political parties have contested and he got approval of his party to contest in the election. Likewise AIADMK approved a candidate and the DMK also approved a candidate and two other independents also contested for this position.

Though it is reserved for SC, he never considered that he is contesting the election to represent SC and hence he approached all caste Hindu community leaders. Since his father had built up a reputation to his family that he was beyond community, people belonging to other communities believed him and chosen him as their candidate. His father's reputation, his wife's service to the sick persons in the villages and his services along with his broader outlook on communal matters helped him to win the election.

He had rich experience in management of cooperative society as he held director position and also in cooperative milk society. He had faced many problems in the organisation from the caste Hindus and his own community. Yet he has not earned any bad name. As he exhibited his dealings openly nobody suspected him. But it took a long time to win the confidence of the caste Hindu collectivities. It is his nature that he won't spend much money for the electioneering because he considered it as a service and for which one should not spend money.

As a president of the Gram Panchayat he used to meet the people in the morning hours and get their complaints. He used to go to the office of the Gram Panchayat every day and discuss with ward members about the petitions and problems of the people. Further he used to verify the accounts and sometimes he himself did write the accounts. On alternative days he visits Panchayat union office to get things done there. He makes visits to various offices in connection with the petitions given by the people. His visits to various offices need not necessarily be a visit to get petitions of the people and sometimes he makes visits to get information about their activities. When officials make visits, he makes all arrangements for the meetings of the officials.

In his Gram Panchayat jurisdiction he has thirty-two hamlets. He said that maintenance of hand pumps, overhead tanks, electric motors, pipelines, street lights, drainage are the major responsibilities of the Panchayat at present. Maintenance of roads footpath, removal of unwanted bushes, construction of walls to avoid soil erosion are the major activities demanded by the people. He stated that the demands of the people have increased many times and the opportunities in the villages have not that much resources to meet them.

He felt that the people have not cooperated with him in tax collection. People are not interested in paying their house tax. Panchayat's main income is house tax. There are several reasons for their refusal to pay the house tax. Most of them felt that it is unnecessary burden on them as their earning is meagre. Some of them feel that the village panchayati president should not involve himself in tax collection. People have been oriented towards non-payment of not only tax but also loans. This practice has been supported by the political parties. Hence they are reluctant to pay the house tax. The expenditure of the Panchayat has to be met from the house tax. Major portion of money goes to salary of the staff and electricity bill.

There are adequate natural resources which have the capacity to yield in lakhs to the Panchayat but they are not maintained well. Near about two hundred acres of forest lands were handed over to Panchayat. If the forest lands are well maintained village Panchayat need not expect money from any other organisation. The commons will yield huge amount of money.

Vadugambadi Panchayat has nine members and of them two are women. President of the village has not aligned with any group during the eve of election as the candidates have grouped themselves into three segments. Vice-president has been elected from the caste Hindu group. Vice-president is always cooperative and supportive to all measures taken by the president. Sofar they have conducted five meetings of Gram Panchayat council. All the members have attended all the meetings without fail and articulated the grievances of the people from their respective wards. In the Panchayat Council meeting the members without any difference of opinion expressed their demands. Especially the caste Hindus have conducted themselves in a dignified way by allowing the other SC members to speak and articulate their grievances. Caste Hindu ward members are highly cooperative to conduct the proceedings smoothly.

The following issues have been projected in the meetings:

a. Providing street light to all the hamlets;
b. Encroachment of a big tank by the landlords has to be evicted;
c. Providing transport facilities to other hamlets;
d. Formation of new roads and maintenance of the roads;
e. Steps to get JVVT grant;
f. Selection of the beneficiaries for the group house scheme;
g. Digging a well for drinking water supply;
h. Extension of water supply pipeline;
i. Construction of checkdam and TV room;
j. Construction of school building;
k. Purchase of street light equipments;

l. IRDP beneficiary selection;
m. Electric motor repair;
n. Road maintenance; and
o. Getting approval for expenditure.

Activities carried out in the Panchayats

The following works have been carried out in the Panchayat area:

1.	JVVT Scheme for group houses	Rs. 5,15,000.00
2.	EAS thittam	Rs. 4,96,000.00
3.	Drought relief work	Rs. 22,05,000.00
4.	Jeevandhara programme	Rs. 80.000.00
5.	State Government Fund	Rs. 2,53,000.00
	Total	Rs. 35,49,000.00

IRDP beneficiaries have been selected by a special meeting based on the recommendation of the ward members. 50% of them are drawn from the SC and the rest are drawn from the non-SC group. It is a well known fact that the beneficiaries for the government schemes have to be selected only in the Gram Sabha. But in reality nobody follows and even the officials do not insist that the beneficiaries are to be selected in Gram Sabha.

Monthly once Panchayat union conducts a meeting to review the Gram Panchayat and Panchayat union works in the villages. All the works are technically estimated by the union and the works are carried out as per the guidelines of the union. The linkages between the Gram Panchayat and Panchayat union is mandatory. Yet the relationship and its outcome depends upon how best the president is able to have good rapport with officials and elected leaders in the union councils. As he had rich experience in the previous period, he developed a good rapport with the officials in the block development office and thus he is able to get things done in the Panchayat union office.

It cannot be the same in all offices. His relationship with Electricity Board is negative. His pleas and beseeches have not evoked any response from the officials of E.B. Though E.B. comes under the purview of panchayats, the officials do not care for the petitions. Likewise the other offices negated the proposals. The officials are indifferent towards his request. Very few officials are cooperative with the elected representatives. Others exhibit animosity towards the leaders as if they have usurped their powers. Officials who have to supervise have not visited the work spot.

There is no contact between the village Panchayat and district Panchayat. He in fact does not know the linkages between the two. Major problems which he faces in the villages are as follows:

a. Jeevandhara grant is not sufficient to meet the requirements of thirty-two hamlets;
b. Electricity facilities have not extended to all hamlets when a few hamlets are getting this facility, other hamlets feel that they are deprived of this facility.
c. Drainage facility is not adequate and we need an appropriate technology for it. For drainage in the village more than money, technology is needed;
d. For maintenance of hand pumps, overhead tank, motors, funds are not adequate;
e. Houses have been provided to SC through the government scheme. For non-SC in the same economic category, we have to provide housing facilities and for which a scheme is needed;
f. Village tanks are with the forest department and

these tanks are to be handed over to the village Panchayat. Government should take necessary step in this regard;

g. Despite the attempts of the village Panchayat, drinking water facilities have not been provided to all the hamlets. If water supply is provided to all the hamlets it is the biggest achievement of the village Panchayat; and

h. Likewise laying road to all hamlets is yet another problem the Panchayat is facing.

Perumal sincerely and religiously feel that providing services and facilities is the main function of the Gram Panchayats. Article 243(G) has not been seriously considered either by the elected leaders or by the officials who work under Panchayats. He felt that the officials are indifferent towards the elected leaders of the Panchayats. MLAs and MPs have been treated with dignity in all local body offices. But the local body leaders have been treated by the officials with contempt. Local body leaders as per his opinion are in need of training unless otherwise local body leaders could not function effectively. Training should be conducted not by the officials but by the academicians and well trained NGOs. The cumbersome administrative procedures made the leaders nervous.

Officials have conducted the training programme in the beginning but the coverage has been very limited namely: a) account system; b) official procedures; and c) micro level planning. They have distributed many small booklets as rules book to follow. In his opinion there is a perception gap between the basic objectives of the decentralization of power and the actual functioning of the Panchayats due to lack of training on the part of officials and elected leaders.

For the success of the new panchayati system he suggested the following:

a. Capacity building exercise has to be done periodically for both elected leaders and officials;
b. The relationship between the elected leaders and the officials who work in Panchayat offices should be smooth and cordial;
c. Development functionaries who work in the jurisdiction of the local bodies should be accountable to the local body leaders;
d. Planning process has to be changed from top-down to bottom-up;
e. Reduction in sponsored schemes of both governments would enable the local bodies to meet the felt needs of the community;
f. Simplifying the administrative procedures would enable the leaders to work more confidently and independently in the villages in administering development;
g. To avoid corruption, make the Panchayat leaders as salaried group who are accountable and liable for action if they misbehave and misappropriate public funds;
h. The existing stumbling bloc in the information dissemination process has to be eliminated and the elected leaders should have free access to information akin to development activities;
i. The interference of MLA and MP in the local body activities could be avoided by stopping the grants to them for executive functions;
j. A healthy work culture has to be developed among the development functionaries who work in the local body institutions;
k. The existing financial condition of the village Panchayat cannot meet the minimum basic needs of the people in the rural areas and hence more

resources are needed for local bodies;

l. The existing purchase procedures have helped only the merchants and the officials not the Panchayats. Actual prices of the articles are much lower than the quoted and approved prices of the articles by the government;

m. The State governments big brother attitude towards the local bodies have to go; and

n. Local body friendly atmosphere has to be created in the years to come.

CASE-II : MUNNILAIKOTTAI

Munnilaikottai Gram Panchayat consists of four hamlets namely Munnilaikottai, Ariyanallur, Ponnaipatti and Easupalayam. This Gram Panchayat is reserved for women general. Mrs. Rajammal Thangavelu is from Ariyanallur hamlet. Mrs. Rajammal had an experience of ward membership in the previous period of local bodies. Her husband is the leader of the block in his party—the DMK. Her husband has been very active in the party for the past twenty-five years. She made up her mind to contest the election at the eleventh hour. She has four children.

Since her husband has been very active in his party, her involvement in the activities of the village is more. He intervened in public activities and helped many individuals to get the government schemes. Her electoral victory was mostly influenced by husbands reputation and his party affiliation.

Totally five candidates have contested in the election. Her nomination from the party (DMK) was announced in the eleventh hour by the Minister I. Periyasamy. Minister himself announced her name in the public meeting itself. There were other four candidates representing the AIADMK, the TMC and independents who prepared their grounds well ahead of Mrs. Rajammal. She had to struggle a lot to manage to win the election despite the open support of the local minister and her caste groups. She won the election with a difference of only thirty votes. She said that the whole family members including her daughters have gone for door to door canvassing. She admitted the fact that her electoral victory was more of the achievements and activities of her husband. Till she filed her nomination she did not care to know about the panchayati system. She was not aware of the provisions of the 73rd Amendment to the Constitution of India and the Tamil Nadu local body act of 1994.

Without knowing the implications of the new system she became the president of Gram panchayat. It is a disease affecting the representative system that the elected members whether for parliament or for state legislature or for local bodies, they never had the inclination to learn but they have developed a perception that they know everything and what they have to do is only to redress the grievances of the people by getting the petitions from the people and placing them in the government offices. They forget the main role of the representatives in the authoritative bodies. She honestly admitted that most of the works are attended to by her husband. She used to receive petition if the people give petition in her house and religiously hand over the same to her husband.

Her husband Mr. Thangavelu visited all the hamlets and received petitions on behalf of his wife. He supervises the group house construction activities. Since he has rich experience in this field she felt that his service is needed and essential. Even to select beneficiaries for government schemes like IRDP and DWCRA she depends on his role in satisfying all council members. Office works are attended to only by her husband. Whether the works are in the Panchayat union or in the collectorate they are all attended to by her husband. Since officials are known to him, there won't be any problem in getting things done in the government offices. She used to go to public functions whenever minister comes to her area. For all correspondence reply would be given by her husband with the help of the panchayat clerk. Officials used to respond positively to the request of her or her husband. Her husband's domination has been perceived by her as his assistance to her to carry out her activities. Totally all the activities are done by her husband.

Munnilaikottai panchayat is fully under the control of the president's husband Mr. Thangavelu. There is no SC/ST member in the village Panchayat council. There are nine members in the Gram Panchayat. Of the nine, six are men and three are women. At the time of election members were divided on party lines but after the election the party rivalry has disappeared. Vice-President of the Gram Panchayat belongs to Christianity. Her husband and the vice-president have decided the beneficiaries for the IRDP and other government programmes. So far she has conducted ten meetings and two emergency meetings. Normally two-third of the members used to attend the meeting. Ward members used to discuss with the husband of the president about the problems of the people in their respective wards. Women member's used to participate in all the deliberations of the council.

Women members used to focus their attention on water supply, medical facilities, facilities for school and employment for women. But they are not vociferous. All their queries are answered properly either by the clerk or by her husband.

Following are the issues discussed in the panchayat council meetings:

a. Group house facilities for economically backward families;
b. Poor maintenance of group houses by the beneficiaries;
c. Construction of T.V. Room in all the hamlets;
d. Construction of threshing floor for the benefit of the farmers;
e. Repairing work in bridges and culverts;
f. Construction of retaining wall in Ariyanallur village;
g. Getting marriage loan from the block office for the deserving families;
h. Problems in selecting IRDP beneficiaries;
i. Repairing electrical motor in the pumping station;
j. Approval for electricity charges;
k. Maintenance of panchayat roads;
l. T.V. Room maintenance and operation of the T.V.;
m. Extension of drinking water supply pipe line to all the hamlets;
n. Construction of overhead tank and deepening of well;
o. Maintenance of GLR in Munnilaikottai village;
p. Getting JVVT grant;
q. Selection of the beneficiaries of the group houses;
r. Maintenance of school building;
s. Proposal to construct a marriage hall;
t. Giving drinking water supply to all the hamlets;
u. Establishing a ration shop in all the hamlets;
v. Construction of drainage to the hamlets;
w. Selecting the beneficiaries to DWCRA scheme.

The following are the grants received and activities had been carried out in the Gram Panchayat:

1.	JVVT scheme for group houses	Rs. 2,76,000
2.	Retaining wall construction	Rs. 59,000
3.	Construction of T.V. Room	Rs. 18,000
4.	Threshing floor construction	Rs. 26,000
5.	EAS Thittam	Rs. 1,20,000
6.	Odai maintenance	Rs. 2,00,000
7.	Earmarked fund 1/3 water supply 2/3 construction of small bridges, drainage	Rs. 16,000
	Total	Rs. 7,15,000

To select beneficiaries for IRDP programme, a special meeting of the Gram Panchayat council has been convened. Beneficiaries have been selected on the basis of their standard of living. One-third of the beneficiaries are selected from SC and two-third beneficiaries are drawn from caste Hindus. Selection was purely based on the consultation with the ward members of all hamlets.

She used to attend all the meetings in the Panchayat union whenever it was convened. She has been accompanied by her husband. Every month review meeting she used to participate along with her husband. She had developed a good rapport with the panchayati union chair-person as the chair-person belongs to the same party. She said that she is maintaining a cordial relationship with all officials hence they are cooperating with her. There is yet another reason for getting active cooperation from the officials. Her husband is a powerful party leader in the block and hence everybody is cooperating with her. She gets many programmes from panchayati union with the support of Panchayat union chair-person. She has completed the work of providing street light to all the hamlets.

She is not aware of the role and functions of the District Panchayat. She gets many programmes from DRDA office and in this connection she visits collectorate. She does not know what the District Panchayat is doing in the villages. Even in the district collectorate the officials are cooperating with her in sanctioning schemes as she observed.

Major Problems in her Village

a. A great deal of demand is for houses to caste Hindus belonging to economically poor sections.
b. Fund available to repair hand pump and water tank motor is not adequate.
c. Drainage is yet another problem in the villages which needs the attention of the government.
d. Jeevan Dhara grant is not sufficient to meet the needs of the village.

She openly explained that even though women are elected to different positions, they have a feeling that they are not well equipped to handle the problems.

She is not aware of the schemes available in DRDA or in panchayat union. Moreover the procedure adopted in the union office is cumbersome and the rules manual handed over to her terrorised her infact. She feels that she needs periodical training to handle the institution. She does not know the real implications of the new Panchayati Raj. She is not getting the Government orders regularly and even to get the G.O. one has to struggle a lot. She felt that women leaders need an exclusive training programme to overcome the inherent problems. classes should be handled by the women activists. She felt that she is dependent on her husband as she does not know anything about governance. More member of NGOs and academics have to be involved in the training programme. She is not much aware of MLAs and MPs area development programme. Her exposure to media is limited.

She suggested the following for the success of the Gram Panchayat:

a. Giving adequate training to the presidents in the Panchayat accounts and maintenance of records.
b. Exclusive programme for women could be arranged and leadership training should be given to the women leaders.
c. Rules and regulations should be flexible so as to meet the requirements of the people.
d. Most of the genuine demands of the people could not be met in the government sponsored programmes and they could be met only through exclusive programme for villages.
e. Provision should be made to allocate more amount of money to meet the demands of the people.
f. Government orders and information should reach the leaders in time without any delay and impediment.
g. Panchayati president should be given salary every month as the work load of the Panchayat president is almost a full time employee.

CASE-III : PACHAMALAYANKOTTAI

Mr. Rajaram, the president, of the Pachamalayankottai Gram Panchayat is the first son of his parents. He hails from a humble family of scheduled caste background. His father is a retired teacher who infact motivated him to take up the leadership role to guide his community as he was subjected to humiliation by the caste Hindu people in the same village. His full attention was drawn towards his community and hence he could not continue his study beyond seventh standard. To help his community he was in need of a support base and finally he found the DMK for this cause and hence he joined the DMK party.

Originally his father was a member of the Indian National Congress. He firmly believed that the problems of the scheduled caste groups could be solved in free India by the party. His dreams were belied as he himself witnessed the humiliation of the scheduled caste people by the caste Hindu groups. Hence he changed his loyalty towards the DMK as this party vociferously highlighted the plight of the non-brahmins especially the backward, most backward and *dalits*. He was not only the person involved in party activities vigorously but also his wife. As a follow-up his son Rajaram has actively took part in the activities of the party. They were guided by Mr. O.P. Raman, a minister of Government of Tamil Nadu during the period of DMK's rule in Tamil Nadu.

Rajaram had his political socialisation from his parents. He attributed that his sustenance in party activities is due to his family background and especially the economic condition. He had five acres of land which provided to his family for its livelihood. He has three children.

He had been imprisoned six times for various struggles as he participated in the programmes of party to defy the order of the government. He had established good relationship with higher functionaries of his party and also with the MLA of his constituency. He said that his main activity is to collect petitions from the people and to approach the officials and politicians to redress the grievances of the people.

There were five candidates contested in the election

from the same village. It is a reserved Gram Panchayat for scheduled caste common. All major political parties have approved their candidates to file nominations. DMK had accepted his nomination, previously a representative from Thevar community became the president of Gram Panchayat who had personal equation with Rajaram as he represented the problems of the *dalit* vigorously. Rajaram has been branded as fundamentalist and he has been projected as a revolutionary. His image has been tarnished by the other candidates who contested with him along with the former president of the village panchayat by projecting him as a castiest leader or communal leader. He had to struggle a lot to convince the people that he is not against any community but he is always working for social justice. He felt that people are always honest and sincere and hence they have eliminated the candidates based on the performance of candidates and their parties. Against this background he was elected to this position.

Details of votes secured by him and others are given below:

TABLE 15.1 : **Details of Votes Secured in 1997 Election**

Sl.No.	Name	Party	Votes secured
1.	Rajaram	DMK	1334
2.	Muthukkalai	Congress	910
3.	Subbaiah	Independent	500
4.	Chitravel	AIADMK	480
5.	Chandran	Independent	400

Source: Computed.

He said that the entire hamlets of Pachamalayankottai and S. Pudukkottai have cast their votes in favour of Mr. Muthukkalai as he instigated the people to think in terms of caste. Since he belonged to Mukkulathor caste, he thought that he could muster his support to win the election by using the caste. Even then he could not win the election. His apprehension is that this type of mobilization has completely marred the perception of the people towards politics. People look at everything from the communal outlook.

But he admitted that even among the people who have been subjected under caste mobilisation rationally think and vote for genuine candidates who have service background. He served in cooperative society for some time and he was a lone member raising voices against corruption. This has brought several problems to him. Hence this kind of activities brought him good name from other communities at the time of election. He said that even in the villages corrupt individuals form nexus and take shelter under caste which has been accepted by innocent common people belonging to that community.

In his village everything has been visualised from caste angle. Innocent people are mobilised on caste banks to cover the corrupt activities of the microscopic minority who belonged to a particular caste. In order to protect his life, necessarily the president said that he has to safeguard himself from this onslaught he had to mobilise his relatives and friends on the same line even though it is felt that it is wrong. He confirmed that he has spent one lakh rupees for this election to meet the election expenses. He has borrowed money from his relatives and money lenders. He made it a routine that he has to visit the panchayat office daily in the morning and attend to the routine work of verifying the accounts and giving reply to the petitions of the people and sending letter to various offices. He said that MLAs, MPs are getting petitions from the people and send the same to panchayats as the subjects are earmarked for panchayat. His argument is why then they operate Rs. 25 lakhs and 1 crore respectively by the MLAs and MPs as area development fund for rural development. He told that near about thirty record books are maintained in the panchayat office for various activities. He has to sign in almost all records.

There are eighteen hamlets in this Panchayat. Maintenance of hand pumps, street lights and drainage are major responsibilities in this village. People demanded that the roads are to be maintained by the Panchayats. Unwanted bushes on the roads have to be removed by the Panchayats, establishing footpaths have to be the responsibility of the Panchayats. Since people have been oriented in the past by the government to demand more facilities and not to contribute anything for the community, they feel that everything has to be looked after by the Panchayats. People expect money from the governments to do service. They are not ready even to pay the nominal amount as house tax which is major source of income. So far the officials have not taken any serious step to collect house tax. Now it has been entrusted to Panchayats. Hence the president has to take step to collect house tax. When house tax is demanded, the routine reply from the people is that the officials are so lenient and kind enough to spare the people but the elected panchayat president is so cruel to the people by demanding house tax. The major sources of income are house tax, bus stand collection, professional tax, entertainment tax and rent from the shops. The amount is as follows:

1.	House tax	Rs. 40,000
2.	Professional tax	Rs. 40,000
3.	Entertainment tax	Rs. 25,000
4.	Rent from shops	Rs. 25,000
5.	Bus stand	Rs. 85,000
	Total	Rs. 2,15,000

The details of the services done to the people in the village are as follows:

1. There are 160 street lights
2. There are 39 hand pumps
3. There are 20 wells
4. There are 10 overhead tanks
5. There are 14 television sets

Major expenditure is for electricity and for E.B. alone panchayat is spending Rs. 60,000 per year. Salary of the staff comes to Rs. 85,000 per year. The resources available at hand are not enough to meet the demands of the people. Even to meet the basic demands, Panchayats need more resources. Water supply, drainage, and street lights are the priorities for the people in the villages.

In his Panchayat there are twelve members in the council and five of them are women. Of the twelve, five belong to SC and seven belong to caste Hindus. As a consequence of the electioneering the elected ward members formed two groups and one group is supporting the president and another one is opposing them. Vice-president belongs to caste Hindu group which complicates the functioning of panchayats further. For each and every activity president has to struggle with the groups. So far the president has conducted eleven meetings after assuming office in the past one year. Out of eleven meetings, eight meetings were conducted with dignity and decorum. Members evinced keen interest in all the matters. For three meetings signatures were obtained from the women since they have not attended the meetings. Women members have always projected the issues relating to women. Their repeated plea is for drinking water supply and street light. It is common everywhere the husbands of women members used to accompany the members when they come to attend the meetings. SC men and women members of SC are vociferous on their issues. This type of bold articulations are due to the scheduled caste movement organised by their leaders.

Various issues have been discussed in their Panchayat meetings. They are:

1. Street light extension
2. Removal of encroachment
3. Bus-stand maintenance
4. Road maintenance and formation
5. Cash gift to staff for Pongal
6. Extension of bus stand
7. Purchase of material for street light maintenance
8. Bus stand court case
9. JVVT grant utilisation
10. IRDP beneficiary selection
11. Establishment of flower market
12. Electric motor repair
13. Extension of pipe line for water supply
14. Grant to funeral of SC beneficiaries
15. FPF implementation to staff
16. D.A. additional distribution as per G.O.
17. Purchase of street light equipments
18. Issue of recommending SC families for receiving patta
19. Approval for E.B. payment

20. T.V. Room maintenance and electrification
21. Sodium vapour bulb installation

Sofar his Panchayat received grants as detailed below:

1. State Finance Commission recommendation 8% tax share awarded to Panchayat and by which this Panchayat has got (11-7-97)	Rs. 85,875
2. JVVT grant (24-9-97)	Rs. 98,500
3. Second instalment as per 8% award	Rs. 90,948
4. Earmarked grant road maintenance bridge/small culverts 1/3 for new drinking water source	Rs. 46,083
Total	Rs. 3,21,406
Union Fund	
1. Formation of metal road	Rs. 4,00,000
2. School building	Rs. 2,40,000
3. Hand pump	Rs. 40,000
Total	Rs. 6,80,000
	Rs. 3,21,406
	Rs. 6,80,000
Grand total	Rs. 10,01,406

Forty-four beneficiaries have been selected for IRDP through public notification through tom-fom. Fifty per cent of the beneficiaries are selected from SC and 50 per cent are selected from caste Hindus. To select the beneficiaries the committee consisting of following members have been included namely bank manager, cooperative society president, cooperative society manager, deputy BDO, ward members and president of the Gram Panchayat. The committee receives applications and they are all sensitised by the committee. Lead Bank manager and manager of cooperative society have played an important role in selecting the right beneficiary. President and ward members used to assist the committee and not recommending the names for loans.

Under the group house scheme about twenty houses were allotted to this Panchayat. As the government is demanding 22' × 22' site for house construction, the eligible individuals do not have that much of space and they have only 15' × 16' and hence this scheme has been transferred to another village. Government issues patta in the space of 15' × 16' and it gives house scheme only to the poor who has the space of 22' × 22' which is contradictory and it needs the attention of the government.

Every month the union officials are conducting a meeting to scrutinise the entire records at village Panchayat office. Each work has to be technically estimated by the union. JVVT works estimate, implementation, quality control, monitoring and bill sanction are done by union. He felt that the powers are vested with union office. He said that he maintains a cordial relationship with union officials as it is necessary for getting more works done quickly in the union office. But union councillors are developing quarrels with panchayat presidents. He openly said that corruption prevails in local bodies also. Everybody is expecting money for the works sanctioned.

Electricity department does not pay attention to the requests and complaints of the Gram Panchayat presidents. Village Panchayat presidents are threatened by the officials. They are supplied with a large number of booklets relating to rules and regulations of programmes and schemes. By doing this, they expect money from the presidents.

The major problem he has facing in his village

are:

a. Maintenance of village Panchayat roads;
b. Insufficient JVVT grant;
c. Inadequate drainage facility;
d. Drinking water supply and extension of pipe line to various streets;
e. Hand pump repair and new installation;
f. House site to SC and other poor families;
g. Inadequate resources to meet the basic needs of the people.

He said that the Gram Panchayat leaders need adequate training in management aspect of Panchayats. In the beginning one day training was given by the officials which was only inauguration and valedictory not skill oriented training. He demands the following in the training programme:

a. Simple accounting system
b. Effective and efficient management of resources
c. Planning aspect
d. Projection of success models

He observed that the JVVT work is a cheating one as it does not generate employment opportunities to local unemployed persons. Most of the works are construction oriented and for which contractors have their own men and women not from the village where construction work takes place. Though it is not given to any contractor, in record, the work is in the name of Panchayat staff but the work is entrusted to a contractor. If the government really wants to generate employment opportunities, it must permit the village Panchayat to take advance so as weekly payment can be made to the local labourers. Both cash and grains have to be given to the unemployed as and when their work is over. Thus the unemployed will get the due share. Panchayat can do this work easily. He further highlighted that JVVT has to be scrutinised, supervised, only by the union officials and there are only two engineers and two technical assistants in a union. This team has to visit twenty-three panchayats to scrutinise one hundred and fifty JVVT works. Due to their delay in inspecting the work, sanctioning of bill and completion of works are getting delayed. This type of arrangement will not help the Panchayats to complete the works in time.

Resource mobilisation is yet another area to be concentrated by the Panchayati presidents. House tax is a major source of income for village panchayats. At present house tax is very low and it could be enhanced to a higher level and the same could be done by the government.

To him, AIADMK cadre neither support nor oppose and they do not evince any interest in Panchayat activities. Congress-I leaders in the village create confusion and bring problems to him. TMC men support him.

Gram Sabha is another issue which has been silenced in the Panchayat due to various reasons. While going through the provisions of the act, Gram Sabha has got enormous powers with regard to decision making. But it is not implemented in reality. Decisions cannot be taken in Gram Sabha as village is divided on caste lines and party lines. Two thousand members cannot be managed by a single individual in a village.

Gram Panchayat president feels that more freedom could be given to the president to choose the work and implement the same. While implementing more number of works, contractors are getting benefits and not the villagers. People have more expectations and they feel that they have no responsibility. They feel that it is their responsibility to cast their votes and expect everything from the government.

The following are his suggestions to improve the conditions:

a. Speedy sanction of projects;
b. Opportunity for villages to plan for development;
c. Providing adequate resources;
d. Reducing centrally sponsored schemes;
e. Reducing the cumbersome rules and regulations;
f. Periodical orientation to the Gram Panchayat presidents in management;
g. Giving thrust to mobilise resources locally;
h. No joint account with vice-president of Gram Panchayats; and
i. Transferring officials from the government to local body.

In true spirit one can say that really people are slowly being empowered. Marginalised people are coming to the limelight because of the reservation but for their emergence they have to pay a price. He observed that this new system may be able to transform a society over night but it has titled the power balance. Power is slowly moving towards the people. It will take time to succeed since it has to cross several problems. But it is sure to win.

CASE-IV : ALATHAMBADI

A.S.G. Sivaguru (b. 1960) a member of Tamil Maanila Congress, son of a Taluk Committee Congress (I) president became the president of Gram Panchayat in a village where a large section of the populace belong to DMK, MDMK, CPI and CPI (M). He made up his mind only in the eleventh hour due to the pressure exerted on him by his close friends. Till his entry he had not given any thought to the new Panchayati Raj system. He said that he was able to win the election not because of his party or his personal popularity, it is only due to the misdeeds of the Communist Party of India (Marxist) in all the activities of the village. Even in the previous Panchayat CPI (M) leader was the president of Gram Panchayat. He has secured 930 votes and his rivals have got 760 and 530 votes respectively. 96 votes were invalid in this election.

Alathambadi Gram Panchayat has four wards with nine members of Panchayat. Three ward members are from CPI (M), four members are from CPI and one member from DMK and MDMK each. He was chosen by his friends as his family has got some reputation in social service as his father associated himself in service activities through Sarvodaya Sangh for a longer period. In this village, his caste is a minority one yet he has been elected. He has spent roughly Rs. 80,000 for his election.

He perceived that providing water supply, laying of rural roads, providing street light facilities are the major functions of the local bodies. He is not aware of 243 (G) of 73rd Constitutional Amendment Act.

He has been conducting panchayati council meeting once in three months but for record purpose he maintained that he has convened meeting every month. Absolutely there is no problem among the members. It is an irony that the president is belonging to TMC and the ward members are from CPI, CPI (M), DMK and MDMK and yet he says that Gram Panchayat is able to function smoothly without any friction.

He was not given any training meticulously instead he has been given instruction in a day programme by the block development officer what to do? and how to do? They are all mere instructions to carry out the programme of the government. While he was taking instruction, one guide book was given to him. So far he has not opened this book. He has no idea about budgetting and planning for development. He is not aware of those provisions in the Panchayats.

So far he has not convened the Gram Sabha. Without the consent of the Gram Sabha he has selected the beneficiaries with the approval of the council members. He said that it is very difficult to meet the requirements of the people within the budget of the Gram Panchayat. People would raise several questions for which he has no answer. Government is also not interested in convening Gram Sabha. He said no one is ready to face the mass. He informed us that he has given wide publicity to the programmes and get applications to select beneficiaries. Selection is in consultation with the council members. Mostly party members used to grab them. As such there is no dispute over them, he claims.

He has carried out the following works:

1.	Graveyard road development including shed	Rs. 20,000
2.	Adidravida graveyard road including shed	Rs. 20.000
3.	Ponnirai Tamaraikulam retaining wall construction	Rs. 27,000
4.	Group house construction 20 Nos.	Rs. 5,40,000
	Total	Rs. 6,07,000

In Alathambadi Panchayat there are about 32 hand pumps, 173 street lights and 5 overhead tanks. The above mentioned assets have to be maintained.

Village Panchayat has raised the following resources:

Annual house tax	Rs. 8,934
Library	Rs. 893
Professional tax	Rs. 27,604
Income from fish ponds	Rs. 10,835
Income from coconut trees	Rs. 5,925
Total	Rs. 54,191

Under Panchayat control there are three workers namely one panchayat clerk and two makkal nala panialargal and for them every month Panchayat has to spend Rs. 1495. Every two months Panchayat has to pay Rs. 7000 to Electricity Board for electric charge.

Panchayat president has to rely on the Panchayat clerk for accounting purposes. There are three accounts which are to be maintained by the Panchayat president to carry out the activities of the Panchayat. He does not know the activities of DRDA. He said that it is also a government department. He has no idea about district planning committee. He feels that the village Panchayat has no linkage with Panchayat union. Panchayat union ward member has allotted one work to this Panchayat through EAS. As such there is no work for this village from District Panchayat.

He openly admits that corruption works perfectly in the offices. For every work one has to give 10% as bribe. Most of the Panchayat presidents have been involved in corrupt practices while getting the projects sanctioned. He is periodically giving money to all officials to get things done in the Panchayat union. Without going to the Panchayat union office one can get things done through giving money to the officials.

As such there is no work for urnala paniyalar. They feel that they could get job in the Government offices by using this position.

There are certain works which will not attract the contractors as the estimate is defective one. Group

House scheme is one which will not draw the attention of the contractors. Officials have taken a decision to give road work to the contractors who are willing to take group house work. Panchayat union officials are maintaining good relationship with the president only when they are periodically paid for all works sanctioned to the Gram Panchayats.

People have developed aspirations in life and hence their wants and demands are unlimited. He is not aware of micro lével planning. He said that Panchayats are functioning on party lines. He has tried his level best to organise an association for Gram Panchayat presidents but in vain due to conflict among themselves to fix offices for some individuals.

He categorically said that arbitrary powers vested with District Collector to control over Gram Panchayat is wrong yet their activities are to be controlled over by some agency. Presidents should be given salary as it is a full time work.

Alathambadi Panchayat annual budget is prepared by Thiruthuraippoondi Panchayat block office. A well prepared proforma is printed and kept it in the office of the Block Panchayat. It is being issued by the union.

He feels that the present day Panchayat will bring more number of problems to the grass-root level leaders. It does not provide opportunity for the youth to emerge as leaders in the new context. Absolutely there is a gap between the expectation and the actuals of the new Panchayati Raj system. No doubt several lakhs of rupees have been spent in the villages through various schemes yet they will not bring ever lasting impact in the life of the people. Neither the people nor the leaders have understood the full meaning and implications of the new Panchayati Raj system. Now Panchayati Raj system is under the control of the officials and not under the fold of the representatives of the people. Neither the Government nor the parties have taken serious efforts to create awareness among the people about the new Panchayati Raj system.

Whatever the works the Panchayats do in the villages, have to be maintained by the people with the help of the Panchayats. It is unfortunate that even the houses constructed and handed over to the SC community, have not been maintained properly. They feel that it is the responsibility of the government to maintain it. They never feel that it is owned by them. They feel that it is the house of the government. It is not only house, whether it is a road, or a hand pump or overhead tank, for everything they rely on the authorities. People have been oriented to look for anything from the government.

He said that people are getting benefits from the Government through schemes. After the new system of governance came into being, these benefits are ensured and corruption has been reduced and not eliminated. Instead of giving bribe individually president of the Gram Panchayat is giving collectively to the officials who are involved in sanctioning schemes and programmes to Gram Panchayat.

Normally responsibilities have to be assigned to the Panchayats and corresponding to the responsibilities, powers have to be conferred upon them. To discharge the responsibilities enough resources have to be allocated and to carry out the works, personnels have to be transferred. These are all inter-related to each other. What we are doing today, he said, is quite contradictory to the established principle of the Panchayati Raj system. Since Government has allocated money, village Panchayats are taking up the works and executing the same. It is not the panchayat of the people and it is the panchayat of the Government. In every village caste panchayat or traditional Panchayat is working very effectively as this Panchayat is conceived as Government Panchayats. Leaders of the Panchayati system is no way different from MLA and MP. They are also having the same characteristics of the MLAs and MPs. Only one difference they have with MLA and MP i.e. local body leaders are nearer to the people. He has a strong belief that unless the people themselves fight against the evils no one system can change the scenario. Panchayat provides a machinery for the people to fight against the evils of the society.

CASE V : MALLANAMPATTI

Socio-Economic Background

1.	Name of the President	:	Mrs. Kamala Rani
2.	Sex	:	Female
3.	Age	:	40 years
4.	Marital Status	:	Married
5.	Caste	:	Kallar - Backward
6.	Religion	:	Hindu
7.	Education	:	S.S.L.C.
8.	Occupation	:	Agriculture
9.	Annual Income	:	Rs. 25,000
10.	Type of House	:	Tiled
11.	Electrification done	:	Yes
12.	Type of family	:	Nuclear
13.	Total family members	:	5
14.	Land holding	:	1 acre wet land
15.	Party affiliation	:	DMK
16.	Other social involvement	:	Member in local mahalir sangam

17.	Address for communication	:	Mrs. Kamla Rani President Mallanampatty Panchayat Mallanampatty Post Batlagundu Block

Special Information

Mrs. Kamla Rani, a physically handicapped woman has been elected as the President of Mallanampatty Panchayat with the active work of her husband and DMK volunteers of Mallanampatty Panchayat. Her husband is keen in electing her as President with the active support of DMK members. After being elected her as a President, her husband took up the responsibility of Panchayat activities even to organise the Panchayat council meetings.

Political Activity

Actually she said that she was not interested in politics. She didn't belong to any political party at all. Her husband and her community compelled her to contest in the election and hence she contested in the election. Later on she started moving with politicians and joined the DMK party with the help of her husband. But her husband is full time party cadre of the village.

Details about Electoral Process

Totally four persons contested in the Panchayat election including the respondent. The other details of the candidates are given in Table 15.2 :

TABLE 15.2 : **Details of Village Panchayat President Election**

S. No.	Name	Community	Party	Votes	Expenditure (Rs.)
1.	Mrs. Kamala Rani	Thevar	DMK	1300	25,000
2.	Mrs. Susila Natarajan	Thevar	AIADMK	650	15,000
3.	Mrs. Jeeva	SC	Con. (I)	130	10,000
4.	Mrs. Nagalakshmi	Chettiar	MDMK	140	10,000

Source : Computed.

Mrs. Kamala Rani relegated the other three candidates with the help of villagers' support, youths and mahalir sangams. The respondents explained that she spent about Rs. 25,000 for this election. During the election, the money is spent on mobilising local youths, meeting their day-to-day expenses, vehicle arrangements for mahalir sangams and her party members expenditure on food. She also informed that the other three candidates spent about Rs. 10,000 to Rs. 15,000. They used more amount of money on vehicle arrangements and wall-posters. But Susila Natarajan, a rich woman used her jeep day and night in the campaign. But she was rejected by people because of her richness.

The total population of this Panchayat is 12,000. The number of votes available in the village is 2100. After the announcement of election results everyday she used to visit all five hamlets of Mallanampatty panchayat with the help of DMK volunteers. She is a member of a local mahalir sangam. There are 5 hamlets in the villages in this Panchayat. They are :

1. Allagapuri
2. Boosaripatti

3. Mallanampatti
4. Lakshmipuram
5. Krishnapuram

People from Allagapuri, Boosaripatti and Mallanampatti village are mostly supporters of DMK. People believed that she is a good candidate for Mallanampatti Panchayat. Her husband has earned a good name in above said three villages and so she was able to defeat her three rivals with the support of her husband. Victory is due to her husband.

Details about Hamlet Villages

In Allagapuri, Gounder, SC and Thevar communities are living. But the dominated caste is Gounder. Boosaripatti, is a multi caste village. But SC is the dominant community. In Mallanampatti village, Thevar community is dominant. In Lakshmipuram, SC and Chettiar are living together. In Krishnapuram is a multi caste village.

The Panchayat has the following facilities:

TABLE 15.3 : **Facilities available in the Panchayat**

S. No.	Particulars	Total	Good in condition	Not good in condition
1.	Street lights	92	60	32
2.	Hand pumps	12	8	4
3.	Open wells	4	4	-
4.	Water tank	5	3	2
5.	Television	5	5	-
6.	Schools	2	2	-

Source : Computed.

There are two schools in this Panchayat. One union school is situated in the Allagapuri. The other one is a management school and it is situated in the Boosaripatti.

Panchayat Meetings

Monthly once Panchayat meeting is conducted in the Panchayat office situated in the Allagarpuri village. Panchayat clerk is available in the Panchayat office from 11 a.m. to 3 p.m. President also informed that her husband is everyday visiting the Panchayat union office at Batlagundu, to collect information related to Panchayat activities.

The president informed that there are nine ward members in her Panchayat and among them three are women including one SC. The other six members are men. Among the six, three are from OBC and three from SC. In the Panchayat meeting, along with ward members the staff like OHT operator, sweeper and clerk will also attend.

Panchayat meeting starts at 11 a.m. and continue upto 2 p.m. The SC ward members used to speak about their village problems like the maintenance of hand pumps, borewell, water tank, drainage systems and group houses to SC people. The other ward members are not interested in their own village problems. They participated in the Panchayat meetings without any objective. Attendance is always full. They claim Rs. 25. SC members are very much conscious to get as many as schemes for their people. The followings are the major issues discussed in the Panchayat meetings.

1. Providing water to individual houses and additional taps to streets.
2. Group houses to SC.
3. Retaining wall is suggested for SC colony as it is situated very near to the main colony.

4. School building and other facilities should be improved, i.e., toilet facilities, classroom benches, chairs and tables, compound wall, and adequate teachers also formed items for discussion.
5. Construction of small bridge — BC ward members suggested.
6. Repairing water tanks i.e., leakages of water and damaged in supporting pillars.
7. All the members demanded a full-time health centre, because more than five villagers are coming to our Panchayat sub-health centre.
8. The SC representatives came to know various schemes through paper and demanded at Panchayat meetings.
9. Problems of street lights and T.V. (frequently under repair conditions).
10. IRDP loan arrangement.

In addition president informed that ward members are not interested in the meeting due to the fact that they are not personally getting any benefit from the Panchayat scheme.

Maintenance of Records

The president informed that the following records are maintained at our Panchayat office:

1. Agenda note
2. Attendance register
3. Tax note i.e., water, house, shop
4. Resolution note
5. Beneficiaries list note

Major Source of Income

The President informed that there are three types of

income for the Gram Panchayat. They are as follows:

1. Collection of house tax
2. Collection of water tax
3. Stamp duty

There is no other source of income to the Panchayat. Hence the president pointed out that by planting, fruit bearing trees in the common grounds of the village, revenue could be enhanced.

Grants Received

The Panchayat received the following amounts for development of Mallanampatti Panchayat and its hamlets :

1.	J.V.V.T.	Rs. 1,25,000
2.	MLA scheme	Rs. 1,70,000
3.	Earmarked	Rs. 30.000
	Total	Rs. 3,25,000

In J.V.V.T. Scheme the following works have been done at Panchayat level.

1. Drainage system has been completed in SC colony.
2. Retaining wall has been completed.
3. Five houses in group house scheme for 5 SC people.
4. Constructed a small bridge to BC area.

In MLA Scheme, new school building has been constructed for IX and X classes at Mallanampatty village.

In the earmarked fund, we are giving Rs. 200 as

funeral assistance to the poor people.

Training

President has undergone one day training programme conducted by block development officer. This training is not so effective. Hence she demanded a separate training programme for the elected leaders along with ward members in the following aspects :

1. Maintenance of records;
2. To raise the sources for Panchayat;
3. How to treat the drug addicts;
4. How to deal with communal problem; and
5. How to get loans.

i.e., mainly alcoholic persons and caste problems in getting loan from government.

Relations with Union/District/Other Officials

The president told that her husband has a close linkage with Panchayat union officials. Since he belongs to DMK party he is able to get works done. Nowadays his life is fully devoted for the party. At district level there is no contact with District Panchayat. Mostly BDOs are guiding Panchayat presidents.

Major Problems at Panchayat Level

1. Sinking borewells in the villages.
2. Repairing of water-tank in all the villages of this Panchayat.
3. Group houses to all the families of the SC community who don't have shelter.
4. Illicit liquor is a menace in the villages. Three-

fourth of the population is consuming the same. Police is also encouraging the same as they will get money illegally. Nobody knows the solution to this in the absence of a government policy.

5. Educated women are large in number in this Panchayat. They are not getting any employment even at the minimum wage. There are women who know typewriting tailoring, teaching and yet they do not find gainful employment opportunity.

Women Members Functioning

Women members are facing lot of problems in the Panchayat. The male members do not cooperate with elected women ward members. It is generally a difficult task for women to attend to both household works and social services. The officials have not recognised the women leaders. Therefore adequate training has to be provided especially to the elected women in the leadership aspects. In addition, our higher officials should also be given training.

Village Plan Exercises

Now, we are planning according to the schemes and money allocation for the needs of our village. But we have not plan for the entire villages. The respondent felt that the Panchayat members and herself need a more awareness and skill for village level planning.

For a Successful Panchayat

President simply suggested that without adequate resources we could not see a successful Panchayat.

Gram Sabha Meeting

Our ward members have informed that the Panchayat

meetings can also be considered as the Gram Sabha meeting. President suggested that conducting Gram Sabha meeting is difficult due to each village have different opinions and expectations. Besides Panchayat finance is not adequate to share the available funds to all those villages. Besides, people participation is very poor due to their personal interests and occupations.

Bank Accounts and Operation

The bank account is jointly operated by both president and vice-president. We have three types of accounts as follows :

1. General accounts
2. Tax accounts
3. Scheme accounts

Panchayat Books, G.O. related with Panchayats

The Panchayat president said that she has only one book namely "Tamil Nadu Panchayati Raj Act 1994" given by Panchayat union. Still now she has not seen any government orders related to Panchayats.

CASE - VI : SITHAREVU

Introduction

Sitharevu village Panchayat is a heterogeneous and multi hamlet (12 nos.) village. The village Panchayat is called in the name of the single hamlet "Sitharevu". The Sitharevu village Panchayat has five wards from which fifteen members have been elected. The categories of the village Panchayat ward members are as follows :

TABLE 15.4 : **Details of Village Panchayat Members**

S.No.	Members	SC category	Other category
1.	Women	2	3
2.	Men	2	8
	Total	4	11

Source : Computed.

The President : Mr. Raja Mohammed is the president, hailing from the Muslim community. Basically he is an entrepreneur owning a lorry. He is a young man involved in political party - DMK. He is a liberal Muslim, having very good rapport with other communities. His father is working as a checking inspector in the government transport corporation. He is doing farming also. He served as the president of local milk cooperative society.

Electoral Process

The village total votes are about 8000 and the respondent got 2500 votes. In Sitharevu there are about 900 votes of minority Muslim community and the respondent has not been elected as a community leader. He secured about 1600 votes from other communities, i.e., 2/3 of his votes from other communities. It shows that he is secular leader not a caste or communal leader. The next candidate got 1980 votes is belonging to Nadar community. And there was a third candidate belonging to Christian community got 1600 votes.

One caste group named Mutharaiyer, one of the dominant caste of Sitharevu hamlet, with the support of marginalised castes put a caste candidate. But he was defeated. The respondent informed that there were six candidates including him in the fray and about four lakh rupees were spent by all of them. The respondent alone spent around one lakh fifty thousand rupees. It is further told that the respondent could gather votes by mobilising people in certain hamlets by offering money for voters of a few community purposes like construction of new temple, renovation and maintenance of temples. He did not bribe the individual voters. But his main rivals strategy was to approach individual voters and offer money, liquor and non-vegetarian feasts. The rivals of the respondent had also played the community card because of the religious background of the president.

The interesting development of the Panchayat electoral process was that the Muthariyar community's youth mandram changed into a unit of National Political Party - BJP. After the election result was declared, the defeated candidates with newly formed BJP unit friends, tried to mobilise local people against the successful election of the respondent. They levelled charges of misbehaviour by Sri Raja Mohammed in the electoral process. He could take oath of office by police protection. The electoral process has created division among the voters on the basis of caste, religion and territory.

Scope for Gram Sabha

The president feels that as he represents only 25% of the total voters who constitute the Gram Sabha, he fears that 75% of the voters who did not vote for him and who are under the influence of different conflicting caste and regional groups might make the functioning of Gram Sabha very difficult. Because of limited resources the demands of different territorial groups could not be met immediately. And so the conflicts over allocation of resources are inevitable. He further feels that the Gram Sabha meeting could be hijacked by certain lumpen elements for their personal and political interests. Genuine members of the Gram Sabha may find it difficult to express their voice in such an atmosphere. Another important point he highlighted here is that under present social condition participation of Harijan in open Gram Sabha meetings in equal footing with other dominant caste groups is almost impossible. In the name of Gram Sabha meeting a few dominant persons and caste groups may try to blackmail the president.

However he feels Gram Sabha meetings can be conducted if it is convened by government officials under prior permission from the district collector. The agenda of meetings may be proposed by the government officials with the concurrence of village Panchayat members, for smooth Gram Sabha proceedings. He also dealt with the problem of mass gathering. The total members of Sitharevu village Panchayat is about 12,000 and the prescribed 1/3 quorum is around 4000 and it is very difficult to bring 4000 people in a particular place. It is inferred that the existence of more groups which may represent different conflicting interests which may prevent consensus from emerging during the Gram Sabha. He suggested that hamlet level Sabhas are ideal for smooth functioning of these direct democratic institutions.

Local Resource Mobilization

House tax is the most potential source of mobilization of resources of Panchayati Raj. House tax in the villages ranges from Rs. 3.50 to Rs. 45.00. He says a building worth of Rs. 1,20,000 is taxed only for Rs. 45 per six month. He feels house tax collection can be increased to 10 times easily. But such hardship of increasing of house tax cannot be taken by Panchayat as he fears resistance from tax payers will be very high and functioning of the village Panchayat will be very much disturbed. He suggested that some scientific method of fixing house taxes for different categories of houses can be calculated at state level and levied by the state government and collected through Panchayat to enhance the income of village Panchayat.

Village Panchayat Meetings

The village Panchayat meetings are regularly conducted as per the procedures prescribed. Most of the members are cooperative and attending the meeting regularly. One or two members who contested election in alliance with the defeated candidates for presidentship are not able to forget the election rivalries. Particularly the vice-president considers the president as the political rivalry and tried to put hurdles in the smooth functioning of village Panchayat meetings. As per the G.O. the vice-president is given the power to hold joint account of village Panchayat in bank. To draw money from village Panchayat account both president and vice-president have to sign in the cheque. This provision gives an impression that vice-president can share the powers with village Panchayat president and he can control the activities of village Panchayat along with the president. However the president of the village Panchayat manipulated the rule and by which a senior member of village Panchayat as the joint account holder. This frustrated the vice-president and he is refusing to cooperate with the president. As the majority of the members are positive and open minded and so the respondent informed that the village Panchayat meetings and activities are smoothly conducted.

Encroachment of Properties of Village Panchayat

Large scale of the properties of village Panchayat were found in this village in the hands of the private individuals. Most of the encroachments are for the following three purposes :

1. For household purposes
2. Encroachment of peramboke lands/irrigation tanks
3. Construction and establishment of shops, business and trade.

The president admits that he is not able to clear certain encroachments which create problems for general public. Encroachment by residence over streets and public property is considered as an inevitable evil. Encroachment in streets affects the sanitary condition of the village to a great extent by preventing construction and ensure maintenance of drainage. Such encroachments affects the drainage of house water and waste water. So water logging is the major problem in the village and become a source of communicable diseases.

Prime commercial lands near bus station and market place are encroached by individuals for personal gains at the cost of public interest. Number of unauthorised shops in streets are found in villages. When the president took some initiatives to remove such encroachments he could not get the support of public or the support of the local police, as the encroachers could gather support from the respective community groups the president could not take strong steps to remove encroachments. However he could successfully removed them from a small irrigation tank. The encroachers determined to physically attack the president. Against this background the president feels that the responsibility of removing such encroachments must be done by the revenue department. Generally the encroachers are well connected with the rural elites and they are able to mobilise people in support of them in case of any eviction process was started by village Panchayat. It is the personal experience of the president that the local police as well the revenue officials are very reluctant to come forward to help the Panchayat in removing the encroachments.

The Schemes and Programmes

The following programmes funded by government were implemented in the village :

I. JVVT

Bridges 4 Nos. at the cost of	56,000/-
	50,000/-
	30,000/-
	20,000/-
A passenger shed 1 No. at the cost of	Rs. 30,000/-
Retaining wall 2 Nos. at the cost of	Rs. 60,000/-
	Rs. 30,000/-

Still Rs. 2.60 lakhs are available for the programmes under JVVT.

II. Panchayat Fund : From the Panchayat fund three bridges at the cost of Rs. 30,000 each and a new pipe line at the cost of Rs. 50,000 provided.

III. Earmarked Fund : Eleven bore wells at the cost of Rs. 21,000 each, 6 taps of Rs. 7500 each, three drainages at the cost of Rs. 30,000 each, 42 nos. of new street lights at the cost of Rs. 3500 each were provided.

A metal road at the cost of Rs. 1,77,000 and a road to graveyard at the cost of Rs. 30,000 were also provided under earmarked fund.

The Condition of Scheduled Castes in the Panchayat

There is high level of awareness among the scheduled caste about various schemes available in Panchayati Raj. Particularly the youth activists among scheduled castes have organised scheduled castes. People under Dr. Ambedkar Mandram is in different hamlets. They demand more and more facilities and services from village Panchayat. The village Panchayat has allotted funds to provide facilities for SC settlements as per the government orders. But still the demands of SC people are not fully satisfied.

In one particular village, caste Hindus organised themselves and refused to provide drinking water to Scheduled Caste people living in the nearby colony. Inspite of repeated requests from the village Panchayat president, they have not corrected themselves. Village Panchayat president feels that he is helpless.

In the same village, president appointed water supply attender from the SC to operate the overhead tank of the village Panchayat. The village community in protest of this action gheraoed the president in the village Panchayat office. The Panchayat president yielded to the pressure of the community and withdrew the appointment of water supply attender. The community was given the choice of selecting the water service attender by itself. The local community organisation gave the post to the highest bidder. Rs. 13,000 was called as the bid amount and deposit in the common good fund of the village. Attender who got appointment had given Rs. 13,000 to the traditional Panchayat.

The Constraints

Corruption in Panchayati Raj is common. Each candidate has spent lakhs of rupees in Panchayati election. The president seems to have spent nearly Rs. 1.50 lakhs. Panchayat president stated that he has spent the amount for prestige and not interested in recovering the amount spent. However it is felt that such a large scale election expenditure would necessary result in political corruption. From discussion with the people related to village Panchayat, it was found that there is a leakage of 10 to 30% of the funds allotted for Panchayats. Panchayat officials on their part in corruption demanded money for each and every work. Normally works have to be implemented directly by Panchayat but in practice contractors are given the responsibility of work. The contractors take care of the demand for bribes and commission from government officials.

Maintenance of Records/Accounts

Panchayat president can operate Panchayat money, jointly with the vice-president or a member of village Panchayat. In the old system Panchayat funds were with the treasury at Panchayat union office. Operation of Panchayat fund were under constant control of block development officer. In the new system village Panchayats are maintaining their funds with their accounts in the nationalised banks of their choice in their areas. Now the accountability of the president for village Panchayat fund is very high. The president of the village Panchayat feels that the old system of having Panchayati Raj fund with the treasury at

Panchayat union is helpful for the presidents.

CASE VII : KOTTUR

Nilakottai Block

Kottur is one of the 23 village Panchayats in Nilakottai union of Dindigul district. This Panchayat union is dominated by the SC community. Nilakottai block is located at the southern part of the Dindigul district. The Nilakottai town is famous for gold ornaments, flowers and brass vessels.

Agriculture is the main occupation of the people in this block. Flower, avarai, tomato are the major crops cultivated in the lands of this block. Wells (farm wells) serve as the main source of irrigation besides the river Vaigai and small tanks.

This Nilakottai block is spread over a total geographical area of 237.5 sq. kms with a population of 1,17,377 and of whom 59,013 are males and the remaining 58,364 females. There are 31,042 scheduled caste and 721 Scheduled Tribe people in this block.

Kottur Panchayat

Kottur is one of the village Panchayats as well as revenue village in the Nilakottai block. Geographically, this Panchayat is spread over an area of 151.00 hectares with sixteen hamlets. The public amenities available in this Panchayat include 13 open wells, 19 hand pumps, four OHTs, one middle school, eight primary schools, seven noon meal centres and one health sub-centre.

For transport, this panchayat has been covered with 6.20 km of Panchayat road, 5.6 km of union road and 3.2 km of state highways.

There are 64 tube lights and one fair price shop (ration shop). Also there is a Primary Agricultural Cooperative Society. For irrigation purposes, there are four union tanks and one percolation tank. But the major source is the farm wells.

The total population of this Panchayat is 6101 of whom 3037 are males and the remaining 3064 females. There are 1635 scheduled caste people in this Panchayat.

The Kottur Panchayat comprises of 16 hamlets the names of which are as follows:

1. Kottur
2. Thathathapatty
3. Nagamanickampatty
4. K. Pudur
5. Michealpalayam
6. Senkottai
7. Jangalpatty
8. Avayampatty
9. Suttikaladipatty
10. Kanni Asaripatty
11. Achipuram
12. Innasipuram
13. Sundaramallipuram
14. Selvanagar
15. Royappanpatty
16. Somapuram

The panchayat office of the Kottur panchayat is located at Michaelpalayam village.

Panchayat President

This Kottur Panchayat presidentship has been reserved for women in the last election. Three candidates contested for. the presidentship of this panchayat. All the three candidates were Christians. The names of these three candidates are :

TABLE 15.5 : **Details of the Village Panchayat President Election**

Sl. No	Name	Party	Symbol
1.	Stella Mary	DMK	Aeroplane symbol
2.	Lourd Mary	AIADMK	Lorry symbol
3.	Lawrence Mary	Congress	Bulb

Source : Computed.

Of the three candidates, Stella Mary got 660 votes, Lourd Mary got 1220 votes and Lawrence Mary got 1586 votes. Thus, Mrs. Lawrence Mary got elected as the president of this Panchayat. She is a Congress women.

Socio-Economic Background

This president is 43 years old and studied upto SSLC. She is a native of the Michaelpalayam village and born in a farmer family. She got married to a local person. Her husband is also a farmer. Politically, he is the president of the Congress party at the block level.

Her husband has 25 acres of land with three individual and four partnership wells; all the wells are with motor pump sets. She has five children, two boys and three girls. Two of her daughters got married, one is in the house, one son is looking after the farm (after completing IX standard.) and the last son is studying BBA at Dindigul.

Motivating Factor

The president Mrs. Lawrence Mary has served as a nominated member in the same village Panchayat during the previous period. During the previous Panchayat election, her husband contested for the presidentship of this Panchayat, but could not win the election. Because of this, and also as he was a rich landlord his wife Mrs. Lawrence Mary was nominated as a member in the Panchayat. This experience as a nominated member helps her to the Panchayat effectively, as the president of the Panchayat at present.

With regard to the factor that motivated her to enter into politics, she reported that it was her husband who induced her to contest for the presidentship. The reason is that he could not contest for the presidentship as it has been reserved for women. Further he had lost the election during the previous time. So, he planned to get the presidentship at least to his wife this time and so he made his wife to contest the election.

As this family is a Congress family, they have the opportunity of having good relationship with the local MLA. This also helped as a plus point to win the election. According to the president Mrs. Lawrence Mary, her husband had the habit of helping the people even without any party/official position. He used to participate in all family functions in the villages. As he was a good social worker, she could win the election easily, as she reports. She also pointed out that she spent Rs. 30,000 towards the election while the other candidate namely Lourd Mary spent only less amount. But the remaining candidate Stella Mary spent more than one lakh rupees, as was reported by their president. Thus, according to her husband, his social service, the party affiliation, his contact/relation with the local MLA, had helped his wife to win the election easily.

Panchayat Members

The Kottur Panchayat has been divided into five wards. The members of these wards are as follows:

TABLE 15.6 : **Details of the Election of Village Panchayat Ward Members**

S. No.	Ward No.		Members
1.	I Ward	:	L. Savadan
			D. Kamala
2.	II Ward	:	Julia Mary
			Thiruthuvam
			Sahaya Rani
3.	III Ward	:	John Peter
			Maria Arockiam
4.	IV Ward	:	P.K. Muthalif
			Dhanapackiam
5.	V Ward	:	K. Nagarani
			Oorkalan
			K. Nagamalai

Source: Computed.

Of these 12 members, K. Nagarani has been elected unopposed. It is also to be noted that there is no nominated member.

Shri L. Savadan, member of the I Ward from Jangalpatty is the Vice-President of this Panchayat and he belongs to the AIADMK party.

Panchayat Meetings

The president reported that a total of 13 meetings were conducted till date. She says that the meetings have been convened regularly. Almost all the members used to attend the Panchayat meetings. The Vice-President, Shri L. Savadan is reported to be rendering full cooperation in the smooth conduct of the meetings without any problem. She says that her earlier experience as a member in the Panchayat helps her in convening and conducting the meetings. She stated that her goal or aim is to improve the road facilities to all the hamlets, to provide safe drinking water and lighting facilities to all the hamlets of the Panchayat. Accordingly, the meetings are being conducted by keeping her aim as its main agenda. The following is the list of items discussed in the meetings:

1. Providing street light facilities drinking water facilities and road facilities to all the hamlets of the Panchayat.
2. Programmes of women development including provision of toilet facilities.
3. Provision of free houses.

In all the meetings, the members demanded more number of free houses to BC families. Similarly, the government programmes are to be shared both by the BC and SC families. But, in this Panchayat, since the BC population is more than the SC population, the proportion of beneficiaries seems to be higher among the SC. In other words, since the SC population is less, the proportion and size of SC beneficiaries seems to be higher than the BC families. This makes the people belonging to BC to demand a major portion of the programmes to the BC which is not permitted by the government. This creates problem among the Panchayat members in all the meetings. So, the Panchayat president opined that the government programmes must be shared among the people in proportion to the communities. She also feels that the free housing scheme should be extended to the BC families also.

Gram Sabha

The president admitted that she is not fully aware of the composition and importance of the Gram Sabha. So, she had not taken any step to convene the meeting of the Gram Sabha.

Development Programmes

The president admitted that she is not aware of her powers as well as the various development programmes of the government. Whenever she meets the Project Officer at the DRDA, he directs her to meet the BDO for some programmes. The BDO, on her visit, informs her the various programmes that have been allotted to her Panchayat. She understands only those programmes that have been sanctioned and implemented to her Panchayat. Even in this case, she is not able to identify various programmes, but her husband keeps in record all such activities. What she does is that with the help of the Panchayat members in the meetings and with the advice of her husband, she selects the beneficiaries of various programmes. Similarly, the union engineer helps her by preparing the estimate for various activities and works and also helps in executing the work. The following is the list of development activities (village-wise) that were carried out by the president.

Achipuram Village

a)	T.V. Room	Rs. 27000/- (JVVT)
b)	Threshing Floor	Rs. 30000/- (JVVT)
c)	Check Dam	Rs. 30000/- (District Fund)

Jangalpatty Village

a)	T.V. Room (2)	Rs. 54000/- (JVVT)
b)	Street lights (4)	Rs. 15000/-
c)	Threshing Floor	Rs. 28000/- (JVVT)
d)	School Building	Rs. 2.5 lakhs (MP Fund)

Michaelpalayam

a)	T.V. Room (2)	Rs. 54000/- (JVVT)
b)	Passengers Shed	Rs. 30000/- (JVVT)
c)	Road (Selvanagar to Michaelpalayam) Rs. 9 lakhs	

Nagamanickenpatty

a)	Check Dam	Rs. 30000/- (JVVT)
b)	T.V. Room	Rs. 27000/- (JVVT)
c)	Threshing Floor	Rs. 30000/- (JVVT)

Kanni Asaripatty

a)	Road	Rs. 30000/- (JVVT)

Pudur

a)	Road	Rs. 8.75 lakhs
b)	Drainage	Rs. 48000/- (JVVT)
c)	Compressor motor	Rs. 40000/- (Collection Fund)

Senkottai

a)	Kitchen	Rs. 30000/- (JVVT)
b)	Drainage	Rs. 30000/- (JVVT)
c)	Small Bridge	Rs. 30000/- (Panchayat Fund)

Suttikaladipatty

a)	T.V. Room (2)	Rs. 54000/- (JVVT)
b)	Borewell (2)	Rs. 80000/-
c)	Hand pump	Rs. 27000/-

Avayampatty

a)	Drainage	Rs. 60000/-
b)	Group House	Rs. 160000/-
c)	Electric Motor	Rs. 18000/-
d)	Street lights	Rs. 160000/-
e)	Threshing Floor	Rs. 30000/-

Apart from the above development activities, an amount of Rs. 1,76,000 has been sanctioned as subsidy to 44 IRDP beneficiaries. But the amount has not been disbursed to the beneficiaries, as the process of selecting the beneficiaries is not yet over.

The president also reported that the Panchayat has cleared the previous year's electricity bill of Rs. 17,000 and also the present year of Rs.17,000.

Source of Income

House tax is the major source of income to this Panchayat. Upto the previous year, an amount of Rs. 14,000 per year had been collected as house tax. But this year the rate of house tax has been raised and they have put a demand for Rs. 52,000. Of this amount Rs. 32,000 had been collected till December 1997.

The other sources of income to this Panchayat is the professional tax. The Panchayat had collected Rs. 6300 during 1996-97 and Rs. 5700 during 1997-98. Also, the Panchayat got Rs. 600 from 2 'C' patta. The president reported that there is no other source of income to this Panchayat. She is of the opinion that the fund allotted to this Panchayat is not adequate. She is also of the opinion that the major demand of the people in this Panchayat is for toilet, drainage, etc. But the government sanction only check dam which is not necessary here.

Relation with other Officials

The Panchayat president reports that the vice-president of this Panchayat Mr. L.O. Savadan is cooperative to all her activities and he renders full support. She says that though he is an AIADMK man he helps her in conducting the Panchayat meetings properly and in implementing development activities.

The BDO also supports her by providing enough schemes to this Panchayat.

The union council member J. Amalarani, a native of Michaelpalayam village (from where the president also comes) is a relative to the president. So, they have mutual understanding in implementing development programmes. She also helps the president in getting more development programmes to this Panchayat.

The district council member Sri. K.P. Chandran is reported to be rendering all support to this president. He is a native of Sempatty, a nearby village of the neighbouring Panchayat.

The union chairman, who is also the local MLA, provides all types of cooperation in getting more funds for this Panchayat. As her husband is the president of the Congress party at the block level, he has the chance of meeting the chairman more frequently, discuss with her about various programmes and demand more money. Her husband's contact with the MLA helps the president to come closer with the MLA and others. The president had developed a good rapport with the MLA. At the request of the MLA, the president had joined the TMC party. All these factors helped the Panchayat to have cordial relationship with all the officials.

Training Programmes Attended

The president reported that she had attended only one training programme to the Panchayati Raj leader provided by the government. She also said that the training programme she attended was not useful enough to understand completely the PR administration.

CASE-VIII : METTUPATTI

Socio-Economic Background

1.	Name of the President	:	Mr. K. Muthupandi
2.	Sex	:	Male
3.	Age	:	31
4.	Marital Status	:	Married
5.	Caste	:	Backward—Nadar
6.	Religion	:	Hindu
7.	Education	:	M.A.
8.	Occupation	:	Agriculture
9.	Annual Income	:	Rs. 20,000
10.	Type of House	:	Tiled
11.	Electrification done	:	Yes

12. Type of Family : Joint-family
13. Total Family Members : 5
14. Land holding : 1 acre wet land
15. Party affiliation : CPI (M)
16. Other Social Involvement :
    i) Secretary for Panchayat presidents Association in Nilakottai Block.
    ii) Joint-Secretary for Tamil Nadu Farmers Association.

Political Activity

From the college days he has been involved in social service activities and he has been selected a leader for students welfare association. After completion of his M.A. Degree, he did not get any job. During that period he joined in the CPI (M). Then he conducted so many meetings for the CPI (M) at the block level. The party members also supported him and helped him at different levels for the development of Mettupatty village. Hence he developed interest in the Panchayat activities and was elected as the president of Mettupatty Panchayat by the support of CPI (M) party members. He helped the villagers to meet Revenue officials, and VAO and fulfilled their obligations.

Details about Electoral Process

Already he got popularity by conducting CPI (M) meetings at the block level. The total population of Mettupatti village is only 1200, out of which 750 are males and the remaining are females. After the announcement of the election, everyday he visited Mettupatty village with the help of volunteers and party members. There is no hamlet villages in this Panchayat. The major communities are Thevar, Nadar and scheduled castes. He has earned a good name among the members of all communities and so he was able to defeat his two rivals. Totally three persons were in the fray including the respondent. The other details of the candidates are given in Table 15.7:

TABLE 15.7 : **Details of Election Expenditures and Votes Secured**

S.No.	Name	Community	Votes	Party	Expenditures for election (Rs.)
1.	K. Muthupandi	Nadar	286	CPI (M)	7,000
2.	Nallamai Thevar	Thevar	239	AIADMK	20,000
3.	Periyakaruppan	Thevar	223	DMK	15,000

Source: Computed.

The respondents explained that he spent about Rs. 7,000 in connection with campaigning during the election— mobilising local youths meeting their day-to-day expenses, vehicle arrangements for his party people. He also informed that the other two candidates spent about Rs. 15,000 to Rs. 20,000. They used more money on vehicle arrangements and wall posters.

The Panchayat has the following facilities.

i) Street lights - 35
ii) Hand pumps - 4
iii) Open wells - 2
iv) Water tank - 1
v) Televisions - 2

(Colour TV is for BC and White & Black TV is for SC)

Panchayat Meetings

There are two types of Panchayat meetings they conduct and one is urgent meeting and another one is ordinary meeting. In the urgent meeting they discussed about the important works and urgent plans. In the ordinary meeting they discussed about the basic facilities of the Panchayat. The president is available in the Panchayat office from 10 a.m. to 2.00 p.m. President also informed that there are six ward members among them three are women including one SC and others are men and all from OBC. The vice-president is an aged man, and cooperating with the president during the deliberations of the Panchayat meetings.

The following are the major issues discussed in the Panchayat meetings:

- problems of street lights about 1/3 of total lights
- drainage system
- repairing of Televisions very often
- employment opportunities to the rural youth
- bus facilities
- absence of health centres
- maintenance of hand pumps
- selection of IRDP beneficiaries

The president informed that monthly once Panchayat meeting will be conducted with the help of the ward members. Two members are not cooperating with president for all the activities due to caste feelings.

Whereas another member belonging to Thevar community is also not cooperating with the president. In the Panchayat meetings 167 important resolutions have been passed. Out of which 67 resolutions akin to major issues and they are all solved and the remainings are not solved. People expect that the village Panchayat must involve in regularising the public distribution system but the respondent felt that he is not the sole authority to do the same.

Implementation of Development Programmes

The selection of beneficiaries is a problematic one. For example president selected certain individuals while party members, and village leaders recommended certain beneficiaries. Totally it was a confusion, hence the president determined that this selection has to be made in future by selecting the eligible candidates without considering political recommendations.

Grants Received

The Panchayat received the following amounts for development of Mettupatty village.

JVVT	-	Rs. 28,000
Jeevan Dhara	-	Rs. 10,000
Earmarked	-	Rs. 5,628

Scheme Works

JVVT

Strengthening the bank of ponds/tanks
Retaining wall
Small culvert

Jeevan Dhara

Only one beneficiary. The selection is not yet done.

Earmarked Fund

The president informed that the maintenance work on the street lights are looked after by a local person under a private arrangement between the president and the local person. The amount spent by him will be reimbursed after receiving the fund from the Panchayat union office.

Major Source of Income

The source of income are as follows:

i) House Tax, ii) Professional Tax, iii) Rent from the shops.

Besides there are 25 coconut trees belonging to village Panchayat. The yield is now enjoyed by the village people. Out of 1000 coconuts from the harvest in every 40 days about 200 coconuts are only given to Panchayat. The president informed that he was trying to get more out of this common property, but in vain.

Linkages with Union/District and other Government Departments

He pointed out that, there is no effective relationships between the union ward members and Panchayat ward members. Besides, the development schemes of the union are not properly intimated to the village Panchayat. Similarly there is also no relationship between village and district Panchayats. Hence the president suggested that, the above said problems to be avoided in the future.

Maintenance of Records

He informed that the following records have been maintained by Panchayat :

1. Attendance Register
2. Salary Register
3. Tax note
4. Bill book
5. Beneficiaries list note
6. JVVT schemes note

In the attendance register, the following members are signed every day. i.e.,

i)	Panchayat clerk	-	Salary Rs. 350
ii)	Panchayat sweeper	-	Salary Rs. 250
iii)	OHT Operator	-	Salary Rs. 275

Training

The president has undergone training conducted by block development officer. This training is not so effective. Hence he pointed out that separate training programme is essential to the elected leaders along with ward members.

For Successful Panchayat

The following are the expectations of the president of village Panchayat:

1. Upgrading the existing primary school to middle school.
2. The educated young women of the SC community are expecting new employment opportunities other than agriculture.
3. The Tamil Nadu State allocation to Panchayati Raj institutions must be enhanced as the other states like West Bengal and Kerala have done.
4. The ward members are interested in developing their kith and kins. And so Grama Sabha meeting

must be conducted in which the selection of beneficiaries and schemes can be fairly done.

5. The Panchayat Presidents have to be elected on the basis of education, experiences and training.
6. Periodical training programme have to be conducted to the Panchayati Raj leaders.
7. Ensuring ward member's cooperation and proper training to ward members.

Political Parties and their Feelings

The Panchayat has four political parties:

1. AIADMK
2. DMK
3. Congress
4. Communist

Members of the Panchayat are having different opinions and feelings within the party. But they are not disturbing Panchayat activities at any circumstance.

Corruption

The president has clearly pointed out that corruption is a continuous process. It has its own nexus. People are involved spontaneously in the corrupt practices knowingly. It works as a system. Poor people could not get things done in the government offices without giving bribe. Nowadays, the corruption is in the government departments, but not in the village. Hence, to eradicate corruption higher level government officials should take necessary action.

Women Members functioning

The president informed that

1. They need training
2. Women social status in the society is not yet improved
3. Educated persons are not helping the illiterates.

People's Participation

In the rural areas people are not ready to participate in the government development programmes, as they feel their say is not respected. Government programmes are operated by the politicians and bureaucrats and not the people and hence they have no faith in participation.

Gram Sabha

It is very difficult to conduct Gram Sabha. The followings are the main reasons:

1. Village leaders are not cooperating the president for convening the Gram Sabha. Besides this they use to support only their own caste people.
2. Ward members are not agreed to conduct Gram Sabha as people generally question them.
3. Age factor is playing a vital role in the decision making process. Still traditional Panchayat leader is so powerful.
4. Besides, the socio-economic condition of the president is poor. Dominant caste group and economically powerful individuals will manipulate the Gram Sabha if convened.
5. Officials are also not interested as questions would be answered only by them. Hence they

also oppose it.

Bank Account and Operation

The bank account is jointly operated by both president and vice-president. They have three types of bank accounts as follows:

1. General Account
2. Tax Account
3. Scheme Account

Panchayat Books, G.O. related with panchayats

The Panchayat president said that he has only one book namely "Tamil Nadu Panchayati Raj Act 1994" given by Panchayat union. Still now he has not seen any government orders related to Panchayat.

CASE IX : KOTHANGUDI

The respondent Smt. V. Pitchiammal, an agricultural labourer, belongs to SC community is the president of Kathangudi. The respondent's husband is also an agricultural labourer. They had two acres of land but they have sold the lands to meet the medical expenses of their only one son. As such both of them are coolies.

Now due to her full time engagement in Panchayati Raj administration, she is not working in the field. Her son used to earn for their livelihood and now he is no more and hence they have to earn for themselves. Her husband works and earns to meet the family expenditure. Now they have adopted a boy from her relative.

The president is living in the SC colony, in the house allotted through SC Free Housing Scheme.

Her mother-in-law is also with them.

She is illiterate. Now she is able to put her signature with the help of adult literacy programme volunteers. Her husband studied upto fifth standard, and he is able to read and write. During the interview her husband had been there for about ten minutes without any interference. The respondent replied to all questions, and expressed opinions freely without anybody's interference. She is a committed and motivated lady cut out for service. She explained that her orientation in CPI (M) and its women's wing moulded her to do social service courageously.

Panchayat Election

The respondent faced a tough competition from the DMK candidate Smt. K. Leelavathy. The respondent informed that her association with CPI(M) party women's wing activities and participation in village affairs enhanced her image among the people which ultimately helped her to get victory in the election with a margin of 952 votes.

She explained that once in a month on the new moon day, the village meeting is organised regularly in which village problems are discussed and solutions are found out in the village itself, avoiding police/ outsider interference. She involved fully in the activities of the women's forum, participated in agitation for solving problems in public distribution system, wage fixation agreement, hike in bus fare and police atrocities on women.

Panchayat Administration

The respondent informed that there are five hamlets including Kothangudi in her Panchayat. The following facilities are available in the Panchayat:

121 Street lights
21 hand pumps
30 taps
3 wells
3 primary schools
3 noon meal centres
2 PDS centres

Hamlets are: 1. Kothangudi, 2. Ayyur, 3. Thozhudur, 4. Thozhudur Madapuram, 5. Kadambamkudi.

The respondent informed that the villagers common demands are drinking water, road maintenance, cleanliness of well and street light maintenance. Problems in PDS are also reported by people.

As the Panchayat office is kept open from 9.30 a.m. to 5.00 p.m., people used to visit and report to the president who is regularly available in the office on matters of service and facilities. Moreover daily newspapers, *Thinamalar* and *Theekathir* are available for common readers in the office. Also there is a T.V. in the office and the youth used to visit and enjoy the serials, cricket and other sports during the day time. The respondent further informed that the officials from Panchayat union and union chairman used to visit Panchayat office and enquire about the schemes carried out in the Panchayat.

The people after experiencing a heavy flood during the last winter, requested the Panchayat to desilt the tanks and ponds. They demanded proper steps and construction at the tank site. The people informed that the income from the tank through auction can be improved by proper cooperation from the people themselves.

Panchayat Meeting

The respondent said that the meeting is being convened once in a month and all members enthusiastically participated in the meeting. She explained one incident of decision making process. Twenty beneficiaries have to be selected for Free Group House Scheme with a ratio of 17 from SC and three from BC. Majority of members suggested that all the beneficiaries can be selected from Kothankudi pocket as it is a big colony and also the next year allocation can be assigned to Ayyur pocket. Only one member representing Ayyur colony refused to this suggestion. The vice-president proposed an alternative suggestion that 10 beneficiaries each from both Kothangudi and Ayyur pocket can be selected. But the Kothangudi members demanded all 20 for Kothangudi. Due to this difference of opinion the Ayyur member did not attend three meetings and made a complaint to the Collector, PO, and Panchayati union officials. The BDO and ABDO visited the president and enquired about this allegation. Considering the truth and the other members' opinion, the BDO and ABDO counselled the Ayyur member and then the 20 beneficiaries have been selected from Kothangudi pocket with the consent of the disputed member also. She informed that she would ensure that the next year allotment for Ayyur and moreover she could request the collector to allot all additional number to her Panchayat so as the demand of Ayyur can be met.

She said that after the flood, the Panchayat did the necessary minor maintenance work at all the hamlets. The rules specification with regard to withdrawal right is very strict. Not more than 300 rupees could be drawn for emergency. This is not adequate, she felt. She further informed that with the help of people, fertilizers have been provided at the tank site steps by putting coconut tree logs etc. around a kutcha step arrangement is provided wherever possible.

Official Relationship

The respondent felt that the union officials are cooperative. She used to meet the ABDO and BDO frequently and discussed with them about the union scheme implementation through Panchayat. The group house scheme is going to be implemented by the Panchayat itself as the union officials agreed to the request of Panchayat. The EOP is also very much positive and properly guiding the president, she told. As such there is no problem with officials from her point of view.

People's Expectation

The respondent informed that inspite of her full time dedication for the cause of people, people expect more facilities and not understanding the Panchayat procedure, Panchayat income etc. The village roads are very long from 2- 1/2 km to 5 km distance which cannot be maintained by village Panchayat. And so she informed that she requested the union to take over the long distanced roads from village Panchayat.

Quality of Electric Items

She complained that the spare parts/bulbs supplied by the approved store is not in good quality. The bulbs glows for about one or two months only. The Panchayats have no freedom to purchase the electrical items from the local shops even if it is economical.

Resource Mobilisation

There are 21 tanks, 120 coconut trees, and 40 tamarind trees. Usually the auction of these resources are under the control of village committee of each pocket. Now due to difference of opinion among the political parties, the auction was very much competitive and this year the income from these sources are increased from Rs. 8,000 to Rs. 35,000.

Programme Implementation

The respondent informed that the demands of all ward members have been passed as resolutions. Works are generally allotted to all wards.

Steps to desilting tanks, deepening of wells, cleaning of ponds, improving drainage system, maintaining roads, providing culverts, constructing TV room, retaining wall, and water supply provision are the major works undertaken in the Panchayat at the cost of about Rs. 1,25,000.

Union Works

Tar road 1 km
Group House 20 Nos.
Road maintenance 2 Nos. have been done

With the help of union councillor Panchayat has approached THDCO and tried to do repair work in 20 houses at AD colony.

The works under MP area development or MLA scheme have not been sanctioned so far to this Panchayat, the respondent informed.

Flood Relief Work and Panchayat President

The respondent informed that during the flood relief

work, she accompanied the VAO and helped in distribution of all clothes, cash, and rice to the eligible farmers and individuals.

She informed that the village committee of her Kothangudi village (pocket) had collected all the money due for their farmers and individuals and distributed the money equally to all families at the hamlet, irrespective of their caste.

Her participation in this work is fully recognised by the revenue official, she felt.

Political Party's Help

She belongs to CPI(M), and the party encourages her involvement. The district level party functionaries regularly visit her area and she used to share her feelings and experiences with them.

The local youth both educated and uneducated, fully stand behind her for helping her in Panchayat administration. She has the feeling that if she is an educated person she would have done much better than this.

Now she has adopted a boy through which she is gaining normalcy after the sorrowful event of the death of her only son.

Training

She expressed that she need regular training in village planning especially to provide employment to educated youth.

A Case Study on the Correspondence received by the Village Respondent of Kothangudi Panchayat

Date	From whom	Subject
20-10-96	Commissioner	Introductory meeting for newly elected presidents
05-12-96	Commissioner	OHT operation ex-gratia amount
28-01-97	Commissioner	Duties/responsibilities review
28-02-97	Commissioner	Drought/drinking water preparatory meet for review
28-02-97	Commissioner	Eye camp
17-03-97	Commissioner	Payment to be made to the highways department for tree auction share
20-03-97	Commissioner	Advise to collect fee from brick making industry @ Rs. 35 for 10,000 bricks
27-02-97	DDO	Street light
18-04-97	Commissioner	Information on DRDA review meeting on new accounting system
18-06-97	ABDO	31 registers maintenance training
12-09-97	Collector	Intimation regarding water supply materials purchase approved contractors
17-12-97	ABDO	Funeral grant disbursement details
27-11-97	ABDO	Visiting of TV mechanic intimation
20-11-97	ABDO	Selection of beneficiaries for supply of tools at free of cost
12-12-97	ABDO	Low lying area identification for housing plan/house site patta identification of beneficiaries
20-10-97	DRD	Intimation of financial allocation

Date	From whom	Subject
04-12-97	ABDO	Jeevandhara JRY - money disbursement guidelines
09-12-97	ABDO	Drinking water supply, cleanliness sanitation/ avoiding of diseases
12-12-97	ABDO	Conversion of village road to union road
16-12-97	ABDO	P.R. Act Tamil Book
10-09-97	ABDO	TV electricity connection
10-09-97	ABDO	TRYSEM beneficiary selection
26-05-97	ABDO	94 to 97 account finalisation
30-05-97	DRO	G.O. 170 received
05-06-97	BDO	Verification of joint account system
11-06-97	DRD	G.O. 248 received
22-07-97	ABDO	Tree planting in public places
13-06-97	Commissioner	Women members family interference avoiding instruction
18-07-97	Commissioner	Small saving drive
25-07-97	Commissioner	Hand pump spare parts expenditure
17-12-97	ABDO	Tax collection
01-08-98	Addl. Director, Agriculture	Crop insurance scheme intimation
01-08-97	Dt. Nutrition Scheme Officer	Awareness generation in nutrition
07-08-98	BDO	Intimation about PA (PD) meeting
07-08-97	PA(PD)	UNICEF/Water harvest project selection of buildings
11-08-97	BDO	50th year of Independence celebration
11-08-97	BDO	TWARD scheme G.O. 252
12-08-97	DRD	10th Finance Commission allocation guidances for fund utilisation
12-08-97	ABDO	To measure the street and mark in the register of VAO

Date	From whom	Subject
28-08-97	ABDO	Panchayat clerk appointment guidelines
25-09-97	Asst. Engineer, Irrigation, Area Dev.	Renovation of tanks - list requested
14-10-97	Commissioner	Preparation for meeting the natural calamities
28-10-97	ABDO	Guidelines to prepare 1998/ 99 budget
12-11-97	ABDO	Makkal Nala Paniyalar appointment/job responsibilities

CASE X : THIRUKKUVALAI

The respondent Smt. R. Pitchaimmal belongs to Konar community (BC). Her husband Sri Ramachandran is an active local leader of DMK since 1962 and he is functioning as the president of DMK local branch. He is now the union representative of DMK party unit.

Election

When the village president position was reserved for women (general) the DMK party decided to nominate the wife of Sri Ramachandran to contest in the election. The respondent informed that their supporters and volunteers of DMK visited each house and informed the voters that as if the president of Thirukkuvalai village Panchayat is from DMK, the Panchayat may receive supports from the Panchayat union as DMK is a ruling party. And so for the past ten years, the then government neglected the village and did not show any interest and commitment to improve its socio-economic condition as it is the birth place of M. Karunanidhi. The respondent gave assurance to the people that the long pending needs of villagers like infrastructure facilities to the schools and hospital, drinking water provision etc. can be fulfilled if she is returned to Panchayat.

The respondent's husband brought the support of the local leaders from the party and they have worked for Pitchammal. With all these support bases DMK candidate won the Panchayat election. She has spent Rs. 35,000 for this election.

Panchayat Meeting

There are 11 hamlet villages including Thirukkuvalai for which there are 9 members (4 women and 5 men) in the Panchayat council.

Monthly once the Panchayat meeting is conducted. The respondent's husband is also available during the meeting, to provide information to the members as those type of works are handled by the husband of the respondent. The respondent further informed that her elder son is also helping her in administering the Panchayat activities. He used to visit the hamlets, ensure the provision of drinking water and street light maintenance etc. At times, her son visits the neighbouring hamlets to find out whether the electric pulbs burnt properly during nights.

The Panchayat passed resolution and sought help from the Chief Minister by informing him that the village is continuously neglected by the then governments for the past ten or fifteen years.

The respondent informed that the members are not properly educated. They demanded the things immediately. Gents in the council are not conducting themselves in the council with a sense of responsibility and not ready to understand the administrative procedures. The respondent's husband listed out the following works that are sanctioned to Thirukkuvalai Panchayat and are carried out in Thirukkuvalai Panchayat.

Sl. No.	Work	Estimate (Rs.)
1.	District Eye Hospital	1 crore
2.	Students Hostel	0.36 lakhs
3.	Sub station of ED	0.30 lakhs
4.	Higher Secondary School infrastructure	0.08 lakhs
5.	Higher Secondary School laboratory	0.06.5 lakhs
6.	Higher Secondary School Compound Wall	0.08.5 lakhs
7.	Higher Secondary School Playground	0.06.5 lakhs
Under DD Plan Scheme		
1.	Union elementary school	1.5 lakhs
2.	Tar road	1.5 lakhs
3.	Scralai spreading	1.5 lakhs
4.	Scralai spreading	0.8 lakhs
5.	Ration shop building	80,000

Panchayat Works

65% grant Rs. 39,000 and
earmarked grant Rs. 20,460
have been received by the village Panchayat.
The income of the Panchayat is very minimum.

House tax	Rs. 7,120
PF	Rs. 12,400
Stamp duty	Rs. 13,000
Mahasul (Tree/pond)	Rs. 2,833
Puliur tank	Rs. 2,500

The respondent informed that there are activities to increase the income of village Panchayat through tree planting. The village Porumboke lands are already encroached and fully occupied by the public. And so tree planting is carried out in highways road side. About 50 coconut tree saplings were planted.

The house tax is now enhanced to minimum from Rs. 3.50 to Rs. 5.50. The income is not sufficient to meet the day-to-day expenditures in providing basic facilities like street light, water supply and public sanitation provision. There are 185 street lights, 22 hand pumps and 25 water taps in the Panchayat.

Programme Implementation

The respondent's husband told that out of total of 18 IRDP allocation, 4 SC and 14 BC are selected. He claimed that the ruling DMK does not influence in the selection. All party people views are accepted and the eligible beneficiaries belonging to all parties are selected. He further informed that the numbers are not sufficient. At least there must be a time target to reach all the poor families who are below the poverty line, he suggested.

JVVT

Under JVVT four culverts at the total cost of Rs. 1,00,000 have been constructed. The material like cement, pipe and spare parts are supplied by union. There is no say to village Panchayats in this scheme.

President's New Role

A vigilance committee is convened in which the president of village Panchayat has to be the president of the committee and VAO has to serve as secretary along with 3 to 4 members representing local farmers. The president has further a role to play in other vigilance committee like Nutrition Noon Meals Programme implementation, PDS and Flood Relief Work. The Village Administrative Officer has taken role as an encroachment to her field and so tried to overshadow the president. The respondent further informed that the supply of free dhotis and sarees, rice and kerosene distribution during the flood relief need close monitoring by the president so as to enable the eligible beneficiaries to get their shares.

The respondent's husband further informed that when highways cleared the roadside, the Panchayat planned to plant 13 trees but the people tried to encroach the place. But the respondent and members tried and avoided the encroachment. But the local traditional leaders and political party leaders did not support the Panchayat.

The people are not evincing interest in public activities. The representatives are also not immediately bringing the problems to the notice of the Panchayat. And so the family members of the Panchayat president are helping by visiting various hamlets and in one hamlet there is no member as all the three members of that particular ward have been selected from one pocket. They give information about their area problems.

Administrative Problem

The earmarked fund utilisations: Out of the total 2/3 has to be spent on road and 1/3 has to be spent on drinking water. The officials are pressing the Panchayat to utilise the fund as early as possible whereas the 1/3 of earmarked fund for drinking water is not sufficient and can be withheld for some time and after an additional allocation or other allocation, a more planned water supply work could be carried out.

Panchayat Clerk

The clerk has studied only +2 whereas he has to maintain 31 records/registers and accounting procedures are more complicated. He is not fully equipped to manage the administration. And so a periodical training is needed for Panchayat clerk also. The old clerks, who were once *karnams* are helping in maintaining the Panchayat accounts of 2, 3 villages and earn an amount of Rs. 1,000 per month additionally. His services are very much needed and so he has been booked by village Panchayat in advance.

Union Scheme *Vs* Panchayat

The union scheme works have been carried out without the knowledge of the village Panchayat, the respondent informed. She explained that when a school building work is undertaken newly, there are quality control measures like watering the constructions, and when construction was done there is no assistance from the contractors to watering. If the concerned village Panchayat is also given a role in monitoring the scheme, there will be an effective monitoring as the building is going to be handed over to the Panchayat after completion. Now it is lacking.

Agricultural Engineering Department Work and Panchayat

Under the auspices of the agricultural engineering department, watershed works are undertaken in two tanks. The department officials approached the Panchayat and consulted about the work. About Rs. 5,00,000 estimated works are carried out in two tanks. The PWD works like channel renovation, earth removing, widening etc. are carried out effectively in consultation with the Panchayats.

Women Reservation/Empowerment

The husband of the Thirukkuvalai village Panchayat felt that the common people have not yet changed their mind set. They have to cooperate, encourage and help the women representative. Based on this new experiment only, the future success is going to be determined.

The Gram Sabha

The respondent felt that as long as alcohol is freely available in the villages, there is no possibility to organise Gram Sabha as per the new PR system. But a common meeting at hamlets can be organised as there will be a social control when the Gram Sabha deliberations are disturbed by any one.

He further informed that due to party politics, some of the local leaders are not giving due respect and recognition to the Panchayat and its new role. They want that it must be a subservient to the state/central governments machineries. The concept of autonomy and decentralised power to the village Panchayats are not acceptable to the traditional leaders, the respondent informed.

Observation

The village Panchayat president Smt. Pitchammal has not grasped the significance of the interview. But she seldom gave her explanation in a limited way. Her husband only plays the role, it seems. It is mostly a proxy.

CASE-XI : PALAYANKUDI

The respondent is Smt. S. Chitra, studied upto Xth standard, married, and belonging to the CPI. Her husband, Mr. Selvam is running a firewood shop. He is also a member in CPI of Palayankudi branch. He is a graduate. (During the interview, the husband accompanied ad relied to several questions as the respondent could not fully answer)

The respondent Smt. Chitra used to involve in her party works through the women's wing. She attended conferences at Thiruvarur and Thiruthuraipoondi many times.

Election

The respondent had a tough challenge from the other two contestants from the MDMK and the AIADMK. The position is reserved for SC (women). She informed that along with the party volunteers, she visited each house and promised the voters that all service facilities would be provided if she returned to the post of president. The respondent said that the other two contestants did not have any public experiences. Wall posters, bit notices and writing on the walls were the campaigning techniques adopted by the respondent.

Her Role as a President

She felt that due to sudden entry into the Panchayati Raj administration without any experience, she could not able to pick up the works. But in course of time, she was able to understand the affairs of the Panchayat. She told that her husband used to read all correspondences and advised in all matters.

Regarding the conduct of Panchayat meeting, her husband does all necessary arrangements and available at the Panchayat office to explain any information needed to the members. She further informed that the books supplied by the Tamil Nadu Government is not understandable.

The Panchayat meeting is organised once in a month and the members are discussing their ward problems in the meeting. According to the allocation, the works are selected in consultation with the members.

She told that the ABDO is occasionally organising meeting for all presidents, explaining the procedures, guidelines and other necessary informations with regard to the Panchayat works.

There are nine members in Palayankudi Panchayat which has only three hamlets Elavarasanallur, Karumpiyur, Thoppanthurai. The three women members actively participate in the meeting, demanding facilities like street light and drinking water at their ward.

There are 120 street lights, 22 taps, 22 hand pumps and three TV in the Panchayat. The members used to raise problem like burial ground road/shed and maintenance of school building. The street lights are often under repair, she told. Further she informed that the income of her Panchayat is very meagre. The house tax is only Rs. 7000 and the professional tax is Rs 1500.

There are about ten tamarind trees, 50 coconut trees and 6 tanks and Rs. 5000 is the income received by Panchayat from the resources. The stamp duty receipt is also a nominal amount and it comes to Rs. 8000.

Development Programmes of Palayankudi Panchayat

Out of 65% allocation JVVT scheme, small bridges, road work and steps to desilt ponds/tanks have been done. Total Rs. 72,000 is received in two instalments and about Rs. 52,000 of works have been cleared. The work is not in progress due to the problems in transportation of material. As the bridge under damage, the transportation is a problem in undertaking development works sanctioned under JVVT.

Under MPs Local Area Development Programme Rs. 10,000 is allotted to the Palayankudi Panchayat. The respondent informed that the allocation is usually divided among the members and spent accordingly.

When there is any objection in deciding the selection, the correct reason is explained to the members. The respondent cited an example that there was an allocation of 20 group houses. 17 to SC and 3 to BC all members demanded the whole allotment to their ward. After a long discussion and debate, it was decided to give preference to the pocket which is located in low level area, where rain water drainage is a problem. By this 17 houses were allotted to SC colony of Palayankudi and out of total 3 houses for BC, widow and poor carpenter family is selected.

The Vice President is not a problematic person, the respondent replied when the interviewer enquired about the joint account system. He is also belonging to CPI party. But he used to verify the works carried out and then only he put his signature, she told.

IRDP Implementation

About 27 beneficiaries have been allotted. The matter is propagated by "Thandora" and mike set announcement. The bank manager, the E.O. (A.H.) and Panchayat president and members have jointly selected the beneficiaries. Only poor families are recommended. The bank manager usually prefer the right beneficiaries as the repayment will decide the next year's commitment of the concerned bank.

The Panchayat administration is done by the Panchayat clerk. 31 registers are maintained at the Panchayat office. The other details regarding the registers are not known to the President. It is explained by her husband.

The Hurdle

The respondent informed that due to her role as the president, her family affairs are not being looked after properly. Her mother-in-law used to murmur on her absence. Her husband has to come from his firewood business to help her in Panchayat affairs. The party is expecting more from her. But the local partymen are not fully cooperating with the president. As any other voter, their party voter are also expected immediate response without understanding the procedures to be adopted by the village Panchayat.

The New Role in Flood Relief Works

The president is one of the member in the committee responsible for estimating the level of damage and allotment of relief amount to the individual for their properties like house and field. To estimate, she has to accompany the VAO and other members, visiting field, crossing channel etc. This is a hard task and being a woman it is very difficult to do so. The queries are replied by the husband, the common people rejected him and his verse that he is not the president. Moreover the VAO is not fully acknowledging her role in relief work, trying to hide the details of payment etc.

The husband of the respondent explained that the village people are not yet recognised the women's position in Panchayat. And also the male chauvinism is more in villages. The women cannot independently function as the village president.

He replied that he would not agree to field his wife for the next election, as the time, energy, money has to be spent by the president. The honorarium announced by the government is not yet distributed. With Rs. 50 per month, how the president can visit government officials to get works for the Panchayats.

And he further told that as they have only one child, owning one acre land, they are able to manage. Otherwise, they are not able to involve fully themselves in public works.

CASE-XII : ATHOOR

Introduction

Smt. M. Jayamary Karuthuraj is the president of Athoor village Panchayat. She is hailing from an agricultural family, owning two acres of wet land, seven acres of dry land. Her husband is a traditional leader, involving in the catholic farmers association of Athoor. They own a tractor.

During the period of 1986 election, her husband contested for president position. But he was defeated.

He took it as a prestige issue and so when panchayati election was announced this time, he prepared to contest again. Unfortunately the position was reserved for women (General). Her husband compelled the respondent to contest even though she did not have any orientation in the political or public life.

Athoor village Panchayat has only two hamlets: Athoor and Old Sempatti. The village is a heterogeneous one, comprising of Thevar, Muslims, SC (Christians), SC (Hindu), Pillai, Nadar and Brahmin.

There are four wards and the total members are twelve. Out of that four are women and eight are men.

Panchayat Election

There were three contestants including the respondent for the Panchayat president position.

1. Ms. Kalarani in support of AIADMK
2. Mrs. Chitra
3. Mrs. Jayamary in support of DMK-TMC

The respondent informed that during the previous election her husband contested. Since her husband owned a licensed arrack shop, meals and arrack were supplied to the volunteers and others who accompanied for election campaign. But this time there was no arrack supply. But every day about 25 to 30 persons visited every house during the evening time. Posters, pamphlets, wall writing were other methods of campaigning. Two days before the polling day with tractor, jeep and lorry, a mass campaign was organised to project her candidature.

The respondent further told that for canvassing for about 1000 votes from Adi Dravida community voters, she had given cash to each voter with the support of party/traditional leaders of those pockets. She informed that her caste people i.e. catholic Christians fully supported her and their family took much hardship in the organising work of Catholic Farmers Association. The popularity of DMK-TMC and her family is the major reason for her success. The respondent won in the election by the margin of more than 500 votes and about Rs. 1 lakh was spent, she informed.

Her Function

The respondent said that her only son, being a graduate interested in public affairs is helping the family, looking after their farm activities and also helping the resondent in Panchayati Raj functions. He deals most of the problem and function as a shadow president.

She informed that she is running the Panchayat with the advice and help of her son. During the interview at her house, she furnished details pertaining to Athoor Panchayat from a diary, notebook and a file, all in a kit. But she is not able to reply other queries like number of registers, correspondences, government orders etc. pertaining to new Panchayati Raj system. She replied that her son only dealt those things. Further the Panchayat clerk is a B.Com graduate and he is properly maintaining all registers.

The Haunting Issue

The previous president collected money from public by promising individual water tap connection. But he failed to do so and there was no account for money collected.

Now, after the introduction of new Panchayati Raj

system, the problem of individual water tap connection was raised. The problem was discussed in the Panchayat meeting and consulted with the local MLA who is fortunately become a minister Sri. I. Periasamy and with his permission Rs. 500 was collected. Receipt for Rs. 300 was given to the individual contributors. The balance was kept as unaccountable money to meet other miscellaneous expenses.

In the mean time an order was issued by the state government, banning all new individual water tap connection created tussle in the village. The problem became an issue and public demanded the money. Rs. 200 is returned to them. The minister could not be able to help as the G.O. could not be violated. The problem was figured in the local newspapers also.

The respondent further informed that Rs. 40,000 to Rs. 50,000 is being spent for proper water supply to the public taps of Adi Dravidar community pockets. Following this the other caste people demanded the same facilities. The Panchayat members also demanded that water supply in all wards has to be improved.

Panchayat Meeting

Monthly once, the Panchayat meeting is conducted. The ward members are demanding a copy of the resolution passed during the previous meeting. Sometimes emergency meetings are organised. The resolutions are not properly circulated due to shortage of time. But the members make this as an issue and make wrong propaganda.

The vice president is belonging to TMC and he is a Thevar community man. The members were divided into groups and so the meeting was disturbed. The members demanded a copy of resolution. Subjects like drinking water, drainage, television, public storage, road facilities were discussed. Rs. 60,648 is the quarterly allocation from the government and Rs. 1,27,120 is the JVVT quarterly share for the Panchayat.

From the union scheme, a number of works are carried out at Athoor Panchayat as the union councillor become the union chairperson. The union chairperson Smt. Margretmary is the close relative of the respondent.

Union road, graveyard road, Mallayapuram road, ration shop and high school building repair are the works carried out by union. Under MP's fund, three tanks renovation and deepening works are carried out. Since the locality is very close to the minister Sri. I. Periasamy's place, the officials are cooperative to this Panchayat.

Her Links

The respondent informed that she used to visit union office, and collector's office frequently. She attends the association meeting of the village presidents association.

IRDP

The allocation is 38 beneficiaries for her Panchayat. 20 beneficiaries are drawn from SC and 18 from BC. Each Panchayat member has recommended two beneficiaries. The union chairman and his brother have also influenced in the selection. There is pressure from the ruling DMK party. But only the poor families are recommended to the bank.

Common Property Resources

The panchayat Porumboke sites are illegally occupied by some influential individuals for constructing cattle shed, houses, stocking of hey, planting of trees etc. Such encroachments are made by the rich families in the villages. It is very difficult to evict them from those sites.

The Political Parties

The political parties are in general not creating any problem. Whereas if any petty issue is reflected in Panchayat meeting they make it as a big one and spread wrong informations on the president, she informed. Writing unanimous letters, passing information to press etc. is done by the political parties. People's expectation is always increasing. They want that Panchayat must do all works immediately. Moreover they are not ready to cooperate with the Panchayat.

The Hamlets

The respondent informed that the society is still male dominated one. The traditional leaders are lobbying themselves against Panchayat and pressurizing the president to fulfil their demands immediately. They expect that the Panchayat president was supported by them and so she must be lenient to them.

Village Panchayat Income (average)

House tax	-	Rs.	10,000.00
Water tax (450 individual connection)	-	Rs.	75,000.00
Professional tax	-	Rs.	40,000.00
Stamp duty	-	Rs.	2,00,000.00
License fee	-	Rs.	2,000.00
Total		Rs.	3,27,000.00

Expenses

Salary	-	Rs.	7,000.00
EB	-	Rs.	10,000.00
Pipe	-	Rs.	2,000.00
Street light	-	Rs.	10,000.00
Road and sanitation	-	Rs.	5,000.00
Total		Rs.	34,000.00

Scheme Fund Received

(1/4) JVVT	- Rs. 65,000	Rs. 2,45,000	(per year)
8th	- Rs. 65,000	Rs. 2,45,000	(per year)
Earmarked	- Rs. 36,000	Rs. 36,000	(per year)
		Rs. 5,26,000	

Corruption

The president informed that corruption is still prevailing in Panchayat administration. The officials are demanding percentage to sanction schemes. But the proportion is comparatively less then previous government.

She felt that the village Panchayat members expect money like officials expect money to sanction the works, bills, and other administrative procedures.

Expenditure incurred from 1.4.97 to 31.12.97

Current bill	Rs.	2,647
-do-	Rs.	49,395
Salary	Rs.	66,345
Sitting allowance	Rs.	2,575
Stationery	Rs.	1,342
Streetlight materials	Rs.	11,895
TV maintenance	Rs.	1,550
Uniform	Rs.	8,076
Funeral grant	Rs.	1,400
Deepavali advance	Rs.	3,400
Other expenses	Rs.	12,342
Earth spreaded on road	Rs.	16,982
Drainage construction in 3 wards	Rs.	3,44,430
Pipe - new extension	Rs.	33,798
Chair/Furnitures	Rs.	5,400
Total	Rs.	5,61,568

CASE-XIII : BLOCK PANCHAYAT

Vice-Chairman of Thiruthuraipoondi Union in Thiruvarur District

The respondent Sri. O.A.T.K. Balu is the union councillor of Thiruthuraipoondi Union. His ward area is the combination of two villages panchayat namely Althambadi and Palayankudi. He belongs to farming community, having a long association (since 1953) with DMK. He was the ex-president of Karimpiyur Panchayat from 1958 to 1965.

Election

The respondent informed that along with him there were two candidates in the fray. He defeated the MDMK candidate with a difference of 700 votes. He explained that his liberal character, public service and his family's tradition contributed along with the DMK-TMC alliance factor which determined his victory.

He told that people themselves joined as groups and canvassed for him. The expenditure for campaigning is met by the presidential candidates of respective Panchayats. Moreover his friends are also very much involved in election campaign. About Rs. 6000 is only spent from his pocket to organise the meeting after his success in the election.

There are 32 village Panchayats in Thiruthuraipoondi Union and 16 union coucillors represent the same. 10 are men members and the rest are women members. The Chairman belongs to CPI party as the majority councillors, 11 out of 16 are from CPI. When the selection of vice-chairman was announced, most of the councillors preferred his candidature. The CPI party also agreed not to field its candidature. Accordingly, he was selected unopposed. The respondent informed that his political background and as well as his other social involvement like trust board member in Thirunellikkaval temple, directorship in TTP Land Bank helped to project his image and so he was unopposed.

Panchayat Union Meeting

The Panchayat union council meeting is promptly conducted, once in a month. Almost all members used to attend the meeting. The deliberations are smooth and the officials are cooperative in conducting the meeting. The ABDO, BDO, UE, PO and the Collector all these officials are very much cooperative in implementing several scheme.

The union councillors are also very much cooperative, and they approach the chairman frequently, get the works done for their wards. The chairman is functioning in an unbiased manner.

CPI	-	11
DMK	-	2
CPI (M)	-	1
TMC	-	1
Independent	-	1
		16
		(Union Councillors)

The commissioner who had joined in 1960s as a clerk in Thiruthuraipoondi Panchayat union has been working with the elected representatives in unison. He is smoothly facing the queries and challenges posed by villagers, PRI representatives.

Works carried out in the ward

Road work 1 km	Rs. 2,00,000
Road work	Rs. 1,00,000
Semi tar road	Rs. 75,000
Retaining wall with step in 5 tanks	Rs. 1,00,000

Group houses 20 Nos.

The respondent informed that as the estimate for group house is not profitable, the contractors are avoiding the work of AO Group house construction. And so, the resolution was passed in the union council meeting that the contractors who executed agreement to undertake group houses only avail other contract order in road work. The respondent told that accordingly the allocation of money for various "tied scheme" has been done and the Panchayat work is carried out. There is no Gram Sabha meeting and public participation in selecting beneficiaries. Selection of schemes are not so serious. And also the mind set of people is not yet changed from the old concept of Panchayat to the new. The new role and responsibility of new PRIs are not understood by the PRI leaders, officials and the people in general. The basic facilities are only projected by the people. Under MLA scheme, Rs. 25,000 is spent for providing a small bridge, Rs. 20 lakh is allotted by DD plan outlay for construction of a big bridge. He could not be able to recollect other types of works carried out by union Panchayat.

He explained the administration of old pattern and felt that the present pattern of Panchayat union without any power and responsibility in the field like agriculture, education, health is not a successful one. The district councillor does not have any effective role in new system, he opined.

The old system encouraged people's involvement, and contribution in village work. Now each and every one among the voters expect some announcements from the government in many forms like always subsidy, loan, free schemes etc. They are not ready to participate in the Panchayat affairs. He cited the flood relief work recently carried out. He informed that the estimation prepared by village people is correct but the same was rejected and the data of AAO is taken into consideration.

Women Councillors Participation

The respondent informed that the present day women

are knowledgeable and consciousnessly living. They are criticising the government. He further informed that the educated councillors are functioning properly than the less educated or illiterate councillors. The respondent informed that his union Thiruthuraipoondi is now standing as a model in Thiruvarur district as the councillors and officials are having harmonious working relationship. And so the corruption has been reduced in Thiruthuraipoondi union. For the past seven years, the officials were functioning at their own way. Now the elected representatives are interested discharging their responsibility. He further informed that the present government and the ruling party is respecting the PR system and instructed the DMK party people not to meddle with Panchayat activities.

Development Concept

The respondent felt that without people's participation development cannot be achieved. He explained that the weaker section of our society is always at the receiving end, and not ready to participate. The middle class has not received any support from the government, but suffered a lot due to corruption, misutilisation of reservation policy and uncontrolled price hikes of essential commodities. Hence they are also not interested in participating in government activities. The higher class enjoys the fruits of development by identifying itself with the power whereas it does not contribute anything. The respondent insisted that the mind set of government as a "big landlord" distributing concessions has to be changed.

The respondent said that the present system of PRI is not a good arrangement. There must be a link between three tiers. He also suggested that the old system could be revived.

He suggested further that the officials and the people's representative do not fully understand the meaning and concept of new system. The welfare concept is not yet changed. The new role of Panchayat as a vehicle of economic development is not yet reflected.

Periodical training, to leaders and officials have to be arranged, the respondent suggested. He suggested that a number of cottage and small scale industries have to be encouraged through PRI. He informed that in old pattern, a number of village industries were organised in Alathampadi village Panchayat, giving employment opportunities, income generation opportunities to the people in the rural areas. Now there is no such step. Cultural activities should be the part of the Panchayats, he observed.

INDEX